$IX FIGURE AUTHOR SERIES

Books 1-2

28 Books to $100K
Backwards Book Launch

MICHELLE KULP

Copyright © 2021 by Monarch Crown Publishing
Expanded Edition. All Rights Reserved. No part of this book may be reproduced in any form without permission in writing from the author. Reviewers may quote brief passages in reviews.

This book is designed to provide accurate and authoritative information in regard to the subject matter herein. It is sold with the understanding that the author and publisher is not engaged in rendering legal, accounting, or other professional services. If you require legal advice or other expert assistance, you should seek the services of a competent professional.

While the author has made every effort to provide accurate website addresses and other information at the time of publication, neither the publisher nor the author assumes any responsibility for errors or changes that occur after publication. Further, the publisher does not have any control over and does not assume any responsibility for author or third-party websites or their content.

ISBN: 978-1-7373222-2-1

Table of Contents

BACKWARD$ BOOK LAUNCH 1

Introduction 7

Chapter 1 – Four Case Studies of 6-Figure+ Author-Preneurs 17

Chapter 2 – Profit Paths to Unlock Your Book's 6-Figure Potential 39

Chapter 3 – Three Types of Income-Generating Books 55

Chapter 4 – Profit Path Calculator 69

Chapter 5 – Why Writing Shorter Books are Better & They Have a Higher ROI 75

Chapter 6 – Seven Questions to Ask Before You Write Your Book 83

Chapter 7 – Publishing Your Book the Right Way 87

Chapter 8 – Launching Your Book as a Bestseller 91

Chapter 9 – Backwards Book Launch Checklist 95

Chatper 10 – 100 Ways to Make $100K 101

Final Words 109

About The Author 111

28 BOOKS TO $100K 113

Introduction 117

Chapter 1 – Why Shorter is Better 127

Chapter 2 – Titles, Titles, Everywhere 133

Chapter 3 – Rapid Writing Secrets 139

Chapter 4 – From Mind Dump to Book Outline 147

Chapter 5 – Seven Questions to Ask Before You Write Your Book 151

Chapter 6 – The Bestseller Checklist 157
Chapter 7 – Your 12-Month Plan 163
Chapter 8 – Self-Publishing 101 171
Chapter 9 – Launch Like a Pro 177
Chapter 10 – Extra Rocket Fuel for Your Book 187
Chapter 11 – Income Goals and Income Tracking Chart .. 191
Chapter 12 – The 30-Day Roadmap to Writing a Book a Month 197
Closing Thoughts 205
Bonus 207
Michelle's Private and Vetted Rolodex 207

BACKWARD$
BOOK
LAUNCH

Reverse Engineer Your
Book and Unlock It's Hidden
6-FIGURE POTENTIAL

MICHELLE KULP

FREE GIFT FOR MY READERS

I have a special gift for my readers! If you would like a copy of the *templates and checklists* I created for writing a book a month so you can generate 6-figure royalties, join my private Facebook group. The FREE gift includes:

- **Annual Publishing Chart** to plan your books for an entire year.
- **Income Tracking Chart** to record your income for an entire year.
- **Book Creation Template** to outline each of your books.
- **16 Rapid Writing Secrets** to help you write your books done fast.
- **Bestseller Checklist** to follow so all of your books will become Amazon Bestsellers.

JOIN THE GROUP NOW
Facebook.com/groups/28BooksTo100K/

Dedication

This book is dedicated to all of my amazing clients and bestselling authors! They are passionate, creative, brilliant, and fun to work with! I'm so happy to be part of their book-creation journey.

Introduction

There is hidden money tucked away inside your book — to the tune of six, seven, and even eight figures! The good news is that you hold the key to unlocking this money!

Whether you have already published a book or you're considering publishing a book in the future, know that all authors face the same problem…

How to Actually Make Money with Their Books!

Unfortunately, most authors have what I call "One-Dimensional" thinking about making money with their books. They naively believe ALL the money comes solely from book royalties.

This limited thinking keeps the majority of authors broke.

The reality is times have changed, and we've come a long way since the days of traditional publishing, where the gatekeepers (large publishing houses and literary agents) had all the power. With the advent of self-publishing resources like Amazon Kindle Direct Publishing (KDP) and IngramSpark, everything has changed.

Now YOU have ALL the POWER.

The question is: Are you going to use it?

Like the music industry, the publishing industry has changed radically. Musicians no longer only make money from albums or song sales. Now they profit in a multitude of ways such as:

- **Live shows/tours**
- **Physical merchandise**
- **Digital merchandise**
- **Performance royalties**
- **Licensing**
- **YouTube**
- **Sponsorships**
- **Session work**
- **Crowdfunding**
- **Streaming pay-outs**
- **And more!**

It's time for authors to start seeing their books as a more prominent gateway to multiple streams of income.

Apple® Technology

Think about Apple. They don't sell *one* product; they have a *SUITE* of products, such as iPads, iPods, iPhones, MacBooks, iMacs, and more!

Apple has what's known as an ***Integrated Product Suite.***

Apple offers a myriad of products, and once a customer purchases their first Apple product and becomes a fan, they typically buy more of the company's products.

I know this because my kids convinced me to leave my flip phone behind and invest in an iPhone several years ago.

I initially fought buying an iPhone because I didn't know much about it, and I thought I wouldn't like it. Quite frankly, I didn't want to expend the energy to learn something new. However, my persuasive kids convinced me to make the change. Now, I own an iPad, a mini iPad, a MacBook, a 27" iMac, and an iPhone.

In this book, I want to teach you how to create an **Integrated Product Suite** around your book, similar to what Apple has. By doing this, you can literally transform your book into a 6-figure and beyond business!

My goal is to help you multiply your book's income 10x by Reverse Engineering the PROFIT into your book first, thereby **creating multiple income streams.**

A book can be a magnetic tool that attracts new readers, followers, leads, and clients directly to your business. After reading this book, you will know exactly how to set it up for your business.

I've been running **BestSellingAuthorProgram.com**, my Amazon Bestseller program, since January 2013 and have done over 300 book launches and helped my clients become #1 bestselling authors! I have also helped clients become Wall Street Journal and USA Today bestselling authors. I love helping my clients transform their books into money-making machines.

One of my clients, Matthew David Hurtado (who is a case study in this book), tripled his product sales in his Vitamin and Supplement Company due to his #1 bestselling book and went from being a 6-figure author-preneur to a 7-figure author-prenuer!

Matthew also launched a coaching program when he published his #1 bestselling book. To date, that program has sold out.

I promise you can do the same if you follow the steps I outlined in this book.

Don't miss out on opportunities because you want to do things the old way or fear the unknown.

Be an action taker and do it immediately. You have the power to build a 6-figure and beyond business with your book if you do it correctly.

Let's take a look at the old way of doing book launches vs. the new method.

The OLD paradigm of a *traditional book launch* is:

Publish, Promote, and then maybe make a **Profit** from royalties. The average author earns less than $500 per month in royalties from their book unless, of course, they are a celebrity or a Super-Marketer.

The New paradigm for Book Launches is:

Design your **Profit Path** first, then **Publish,** then **Promote**.

NOTE: You can implement profit paths into a previously published book.

3 Steps to the Backwards Book Launch method:

Step 1: Design the Profit Path for your book.

Step 2: Publish your book the right way.

Step 3: Promote your book and become a #1 Bestselling Author.

To make six figures plus with your book, it's paramount to *reverse-engineer the profit into your book at the beginning rather than at the end.*

For most authors, the book's *profit* is an afterthought instead of the first thought.

We are living in an Uber- and Amazon-dominated world. To realize your dreams and goals, you must embrace this new world and leave behind the old world and your *old thinking*.

Instead of *hoping* you will make money solely from book royalties, I will teach you how to build profit paths organically and creatively into your book.

Using my *Backwards Book Launch* method, you will create something valuable and critical to your **long-term success** as an author.

BUSINESS ASSETS

Imagine being a 6-figure author and being able to reach and impact hundreds and perhaps thousands of people with your book's message.

How good will that feel?

Being a broke author serves no one. In fact, it keeps you invisible and keeps your message hidden from the people who need it most.

It's time to change that now.

Smart entrepreneurs, including coaches, consultants, software developers, doctors, healers, accountants, lawyers, high-level business owners, and speakers, are using my *Backwards Book Launch* method to cash in on their knowledge and expertise to the tune of an additional six figures plus from their book.

This book contains four detailed case studies of Smart Entrepreneurs who have built their 6 to 8-figure empires on the back end of their books.

I think the consensus among most entrepreneurs these days is that writing and publishing a book is one of the best ways to become an *"author-ity"* in their field and elevate their credibility. However, it doesn't have to end there.

Remember this…

> *People are Inundated with INFORMATION but are Hungry for TRANSFORMATION.*

Reading a book filled with great content and information can be transformational, but only if the readers actually apply and implement what they learn.

For many readers, it stops there.

They read a book and love the content, but often need the author's (expert's) help to implement the strategies outlined in the book to get them to the next level.

Authors everywhere are missing a huge opportunity to help their readers on a deeper level with the book's message. They are doing their readers (and potential customers) a disservice if they don't have a follow-up program built on the back end of their book.

Here's an example…

Years ago, I purchased author Perry Marshall's 268-page book, *The Ultimate Guide to Facebook Advertising: How to Access 1 Billion Potential Customers in 10 Minutes*. I was completely overwhelmed and confused by the information, so I took no action with the information contained in the book.

If the author had offered an online course, a coaching program, or done-for-you services where I could receive help implementing the information from his book, I would have gladly invested more money with him.

At the time, Perry Marshall did *not* have a program on the backend of his book.

I recently did some research and discovered that Perry Marshall now offers **"Facebook University"**, a membership program for $59 per month. Now he has a direct profit path from his book to his membership program! (He actually has many offerings related to his books which give him multiple streams of income.)

Perry Marshall says that publishing his first book was the best decision he ever made in his business and that it took him from being a *nobody* to a *somebody* – a highly paid expert in his field. He said that having a book allowed him to increase his consulting fees by over 500% and create multiple income streams from his programs.

I'm so excited to teach you how to go from being a broke author to a rich author so you can 10x your income, impact, and influence!

Here's a sampling of what you'll discover in this book:

- How a guy who wrote a book about Pumpkin Patches is now making 7-figures on the backend of his books.
- How an entrepreneur went from flat broke to an 8-Figure Business by giving away FREE books.

- How a computer nerd used his books to attract thousands of followers and built a 7-figure business with multiple streams of income.

- How a guy suffering from complications of Lyme Disease used a #1 bestselling book to revitalize his product business to the tune of 7 figures and build a brand-new coaching platform to the tune of 6 figures.

- 12 Profit Paths you can add to your book right now to generate an additional 6 to 7 figures in revenue.

- **Bonus: 100 Ways to Make $100k**

- How investing eight hours per year can add six figures in revenue from your book.

- How NOT to write income-blocking books (which most authors do).

- The three types of income-producing books you should be writing.

- How a $37 per month program is generating $166,000 per month for one Author-Preneur.

- How to add on as many profit paths to your book as you want so you can 10x your income.

- Why shorter books are better and how you can realistically write a book a month.

- Three steps to implement the Backwards Book Launch.

Let's get started…

Chapter 1

Four Case Studies of 6-Figure+ Author-Preneurs

There's no need to reinvent the wheel when it comes to making HUGE profits from your book.

In this chapter, I will introduce you to four brilliant author-preneurs who not only have written amazing books but have built six-figure empires and beyond around their bestselling books, and one of them is a client of mine!

First up is…

Profit First by Mike Michalowicz

Mike Michalowicz is a genius. Seriously, I love this guy!

I picked up his book *Profit First: Transform Your Business from a Cash-Eating Monster to a Money-Making Machine* at Barnes and Noble one day. Then, about a week later, I picked up another one of his books, *The Pumpkin Plan: Simple Strategies to Grow a Remarkable Business in Any Field*.

I read *Profit First* in about a week and was very impressed.

In *Profit First*, Mike teaches readers (business owners) why the traditional accounting method of **Sales – Expenses = Profit** is not just contrary to human behavior but is a myth that locks people into a never-ending cycle of *selling more yet profiting less*.

Profit First actually flips the formula (very similar to what I'm doing here with the **Backwards Book Launch** – flipping the traditional formula) and shows business owners the new way to have a profitable business: **Sales – Profit = Expenses**.

Of course, Mike provides multiple case studies throughout his book detailing readers who have applied the *Profit First Formula*, transforming, and in some cases saving their failing businesses.

I love that he didn't STOP at just writing a great book. He knew that business owners would need help implementing his teachings.

Instead of being the only one who could teach his methods to others through coaching, consulting, or even an online course, Mike created a **High-Ticket Certification Program** on the backend of his book. He certifies accountants, financial planners, business coaches, and other professionals who meet his criteria to teach his *Profit First Formula*.

There is no pricing on his website for the cost of the certification program, but my estimate is it's about $10K. At the time of this writing, Mike has certified 128 people. Estimating $10K per person for certification would be an additional profit of over $1 million!

In addition, he offers an affiliate program so that others can sell his services for a portion of the sales, allowing him to make money from other people's efforts.

I don't know the details of his certification program as there are many ways to structure these types of offerings, but he may also be taking a revenue share and/or a yearly renewal fee for his program.

It's a brilliant strategy to add six or seven figures to your book's profit.

Certifications Are a Huge Income Generator for *Profit First*

Here's what Mike says about his certification program in his book:

"As of this very second, there are 128 accountants, bookkeepers, and coaches working hand in hand with me to guide entrepreneurs on an implementation of Profit First. (No worries. You can absolutely do this on your own, but for some people, having an accountability part-

ner who knows the ins and outs of their industry who can guide them step-by-step is a better approach.) Of these 128 Profit First Professionals (PFPs), on average we have directed the Profit First implementation of ten companies per PFP. That means we have guided 1,280 businesses to success using Profit First."

I'm sure you're starting to see the BIG picture here.

By certifying others in his teachings, Mike is able to reach and impact the masses.

Brilliant, right?

I'm considering hiring a PFP (Profit First Professional) for my business because I really believe in Mike's teachings and philosophy (and I hate all things related to accounting.)

Throughout Mike's book, he is constantly adding value and building his email list by offering resources by visiting his website.

Mike's other BIG profit path with his book is speaking engagements. Here is what Mike says:

"Helping you and all of our fellow entrepreneurs become more profitable is my life's purpose. I am flying all over America and beyond to speak about Profit First. Tomorrow I will speak to more than 1,100 pharmacy owners at an event in Houston, then to 25 people (if I am lucky) in Casper, Wyoming, then over to New Orleans to talk with 200 folks in the morning and then a panic dash (via plane, train, and Uber) to Washington, D.C, for an evening keynote. Then I'll travel *abroad for a few more events. In between, I will do interviews for about four podcasts a day, recording my own podcast (ahem—The Profit First Podcast, of course) and updating this book at night. I do all of these with joy. I will teach this to anyone and everyone."*

Mike has not only built a 7-figure empire around his book, *Profit First,* and his teachings. He has truly created a movement.

***Think about what MOVEMENT
you can create with your book.***

Mike Michaelowicz is transforming lives, and I'm proud of him for that.

The truth of the matter is...

---

*The book is not the end;
the book is just the beginning.*

From what I see, Mike has at least four streams of income (in addition to royalties) from *Profit First*:

1. **Certification Program**

2. **Speaking Engagements**

3. **Possible Revenue share with his Certification program and/or licensing or annual fees**

4. **Affiliate Program**

He has created similar profit paths with his book *The Pumpkin Plan*.

Those interested can become a *Certified Pumpkin Plan Strategist* by application and invitation only.

Mike markets his certification program to coaches, entrepreneurs, teachers, trainers, speakers, and anyone who wants to start, build, or grow their business with a methodology to teach (his).

It's a brilliant approach to building a 7-figure business with a book!

I'm sure ideas of how you can add huge streams of income to your book(s) are spinning in your mind right now.

Our next case study involves a Peak Performance Coach you may have heard of…

Brendon Burchard has the ultimate rags-to-riches story.

Brendon Burchard, Peak Performance Coach

Brief introduction to Brendon:

"After suffering depression and surviving a car accident at the age of 19, Brendon faced what he felt were life's last questions: 'Did I live fully? Did I love openly? Did I make a difference?' His intention to be happy with the answers led to his personal breakthroughs, and ultimately to his life's purpose of helping others live, love and matter. He spent his 20s researching psychology and leadership, and consulting at Accenture. By age 32, he had struck out on his own and become a #1 best-selling author, an in-demand high performance coach, a sought-after speaker, and an early pioneer in the online education space.

"Widely considered one of the most successful early pioneers in online education, Brendon runs an 8-figure multi-media training company. He launched million-dollar online courses in 2009, and he has now passed 17 consecutive online promotions that generated more than 7 figures of revenue in less than seven days each. He shares his knowledge publicly and also privately advises many of the best online marketers in the world via Experts Academy."

Highlights about Brendon:

- Brendon Burchard is one of the top motivation and marketing trainers in the world. –Larry King
- Top 25 Most Influential Leaders in Personal Growth and Achievement. –*Success Magazine*
- Top 100 Most Followed Public Figure in the World. –Facebook Insights

- One of the most influential leaders in the field of personal growth. –O, *The Oprah Magazine*
- The world's leading high-performance coach. –Oprah.com

Brendon has a very powerful story.

What has brought Brendon to that high-level expert status are his bestselling books and how brilliantly he leverages them by attracting raving fans and generating a massive email list by giving away his books for FREE!

He ultimately gives away almost every book he writes for FREE to build up his massive email list and sell products on the backend of those books.

When Brendon's book was rejected by a major Publisher…

"Brendon famously fought for his art when a major publisher turned down his last book, **The Motivation Manifesto.** *This book has since spent over 30 weeks on The New York Times Bestseller List after debuting #1 on BN.com. It's now the bestselling motivation title of this century."*

Brendon's other New York Times bestselling books include:

- *The Charge: Activating the 10 Human Drives that Make You Feel Alive*
- *The Millionaire Messenger*
- *Life's Golden Ticket*

His books have been #1 on every major bestseller list, including Amazon.com, BN.com, USA Today, and The Wall Street Journal.

Over 1,500,000 people have downloaded his books, white papers, and eBooks, and his work has been translated into 25+ languages. His latest book is ***High Performance Habits: How Extraordinary People Become That Way.***"

And guess what? He's giving it away for FREE!

Brendon's 7-Figure Sales Funnel

A few years ago, I decided to reverse engineer Brendon's sales funnel to determine exactly how he was making seven figures from his book, ***The Charge: Activating the 10 Human Drives that Make You Feel Alive.***

Here's what I discovered:

- Brendon did massive free and paid promotions to drive people to a landing page for the FREE copy of his physical book, *The Charge.*

- After signing up and providing all your information (name, email, address, phone number, etc.), he would ship the book to you for the cost of *shipping and handling only.*

- In addition to the book, buyers would receive the following FREE Bonuses:

- Three videos on how Millionaires succeed
- The 1-Page Productivity guide (the secret weapon used by CEOs worldwide to regain control of their days and reach their goals faster).
- A "One Time" offer page with a 90% discount on his High-Performance Training Course that he normally sells for $997. You can get it for $99. If you don't get it right then, you will never see this offer again.

- Following that offer, buyers are put into his autoresponder series, consisting of the following:

#1 – Training Video #1 Delivered with a *Thank You* message

#2 – Training Video #2 Delivered

#3 – Training Video #3 Delivered

#4 – Invite to Sign Up for Brendon's Master's Course that requires you to watch a long video before being directed to the sales page; the cost of that course is $997.

#5 – Another video explaining why you should sign up for his $997 Master's Course

#6 - Final Video about the Master's Course

The above outlines the 7-Figure Sales Funnel Brendon uses to make money on the backend of his book.

He launches the book to #1 by pre-selling the book and having a landing page with extra bonuses for pre-orders. Once he has achieved *bestselling author* status, he gives the book away for FREE to build a massive email list.

Also, when I received Brendon's book, the package included some additional sales materials to promote his programs.

Two million students have completed Brendon's online courses and video series. He is impacting the masses.

I love the strategy of a one-time low offer because, for many, anything under $100 is a no-brainer. He likely makes six figures on that offer alone.

Those in his high-ticket $997 Master's program probably have access to join higher level and higher-cost programs.

Many entrepreneurs at this level can command fees for their private coaching and/or mastermind groups in excess of six figures!

What can you create as a one-time offer to sell on the backend of your book?

Many times, you can re-purpose videos, audios, and training materials from other programs you have.

Brendon sold a recording of a presentation that he had previously given to others who paid $997 for it, creating a high perceived value.

This formula of giving away his print book must be a big moneymaker because he does it for just about every book he publishes.

I recently saw Brendon promoting his book on habits and was giving away several bonuses to those who purchased his book during the pre-order period.

Once the book becomes a #1 bestseller, he will most likely start giving away that book.

Giving away a book that is a *bestseller* is a great way to build your email list fast. *Who doesn't want a FREE book from a bestselling author, right?*

You can also use Facebook ads to drive traffic to a landing page where you give away your book.

It's important to become a #1 bestselling author because once your book hits the Amazon bestsellers list, it's on Amazon's radar. Your book goes from being invisible to visible. Amazon's internal marketing kicks in, and they start promoting your book in a myriad of ways.

Amazon uses an internal algorithm which I believe has to do with reviews, sales, downloads, keywords, and categories.

It's a very powerful system that you can't buy your way into. Amazon rewards bestselling authors by promoting their books to members and customers.

Our next case study is an Internet Marketing Entrepreneur who sells software on the backend of his books. Again, you may have heard of him...

Russell Brunson, The Sales Funnel Guy

Russell Brunson didn't start by writing and publishing books, but he quickly watched other 7-figure Author-Preneurs profit from giving away FREE books, so he followed in their footsteps.

Multiple books with Multiple Streams of Income

To date, Russell Brunson, software creator of **ClickFunnels,** has written the following books and sold over 1,000,000 copies:

- *Expert Secrets*
- *DotCom Secrets*
- *108 Proven Split Test Winners*
- *Funnel Stacking: The 3 Core Funnels and How They Work Together*

I've been running an online business since 2005, and I know the biggest concept entrepreneurs struggle to grasp and learn is sales funnels.

Russell Brunson is a master in sales funnels. He makes a fortune teaching everything he knows about sales funnels, such as certifying coaches in sales funnel training, advanced funnel training programs, and more.

His big money maker is his ClickFunnels® software that currently sells for $97 or $297 per month, depending on what features you want.

I love that Russell is writing books to drive sales for his software.

It reminds me of Robert Kiyosaki, author of *Rich Dad, Poor Dad*, who years ago wanted to sell his board game, *The CASHFLOW® Game* but was having trouble.

At age nine, his Rich Dad taught him how to be a rich man by playing *Monopoly*. In 1994, Robert and his wife, Kim, decided to take what they had learned from his dad and create a game board so others could have fun learning.

There are two tracks on his board game, CASHFLOW® which are:

1. **The Rat Race**

2. **The Fast Track**

The object of the game is to increase your financial IQ to exit the rat race and have more passive income, so you don't have to work anymore, and your money is working for you.

According to the Self-Publishing Hall of Fame, here's the story behind what the book's purpose was:

"Robert Kiyosaki originally self-published Rich Dad, Poor Dad, written with Sharon Lechter, in 1997 as a $15.95 *brochure* designed to attract customers to his website where he could sell his $195 Cashflow® board game.

After selling rights to Warner Business Books in 2000 and appearing on Oprah, he sold millions of copies, with the book sitting on the New York Times bestseller list for four years. By New Year's 2005, the book had sold more than 10 million copies and was the #1 business bestseller for 2004 according to USA Today."

Since Robert could not sell his *Cashflow Game,* he decided to **WRITE A BOOK** that would leave a breadcrumb trail to his game, and his plan worked brilliantly.

His book was an *unexpected* massive hit and sold more than 10 million copies, making him famous!

Next up is one of my favorite clients...

* * *

Matthew David Hurtado, 7-Figure Entrepreneur

Two years after launching Matthew's first book, *Allow: The Law of Least Effort to Receive Your Desires*, I caught up with him and did an interview.

Following is an excerpt from that interview.

Matthew, why did you work with me on launching your first book, "Allow"?

It's time invested. *Who has the time*?

You didn't learn this stuff overnight, and you can't teach somebody how to do it overnight.

They're still going to have to put an ample amount of time to get to where you're at.

I'd rather just employ you to do what you do best (launching books to the #1 bestsellers list) and I'll just focus on being better at what I do.

What has this book done for you and your business?

The book has transformed my life.

It was the best decision I've made in my professional career. At the time, I needed to establish a new platform that would launch me to where I'm at today.

So, building the theme around that book and then the credibility that you brought to the table with the #1 bestseller status really opens the door for me to make that connection with someone.

Now I'm an authority, and I have the credibility that gets me in the door, so I can deliver.

How have you used the book since the initial launch?

The book is like a very long sales letter. It brings people into my world where I talk about some of the products and services that I offer. Because I share a lot of transformative value upfront with people, they like and trust me, and they get to know me through the book. It's like I'm having a face-to-face conversation with them.

As a result of the connection and conversation, they've already decided they want to work with me. So, I've been able to launch a coaching platform that has been tremendously successful in conjunction with my products business. I've tripled my product business in the last two years.

A lot of this success has to do with the book because the book has gotten me into a lot of doors that I wouldn't have normally been able to enter.

I'm not a doctor. I'm not a celebrity on TV, so how am I going to get that authority status?

Well, that's what the book going to #1 bestseller did for me. It got me authority status, and people now think: "Hey, this guy knows what he is talking about." I deliver so much value; it's a perfect combination.

How was your business before the book?

Before the book, I only sold products. I didn't have my coaching platform. I was doing well. But I decided to get smart and leverage my sales capacity using a proper book.

Dan Kennedy really opened my eyes when he said, "Everybody should have a book because it really is a modern-day business card, and it opens the door to many places you would normally not get into."

As soon as I heard Dan Kennedy say that, I attracted you into my life. And I thought, "This is going to be great." You could do all of the heavy lifting for me, and all I had to do was sit back and think about what would happen when the reader got to the end of my book. I strategized exactly what would happen when they opened my book, and I figured out what I wanted them to do. Then, we laid it the book out that way. It's the perfect sales funnel.

What was your free gift offer in your book?

I offered a 10-minute consultation as a free gift at the beginning of the book.

I don't need an hour to get to what's blocking somebody; just 10 minutes.

I learned how the mind works. The first thing somebody says as an answer is an obsession, the second thing is fluff, and the third thing is the heart of the matter.

So, during my 10-minute consultation, I would ask the person where they were stuck in life and five reasons they were stuck there. I would talk about the third reason they would give me.

During this 10-minute consultation, they instantly knew that I knew what I was talking about because I could get to the heart of the matter quickly. Once they had confidence in me, the next logical step was to work with me in my coaching program.

I've sold out on all of my coaching packages because of my book. I had three different packages, ranging from $197 to $2997. The majority of people purchased the $2997 10-hour coaching package. I also sold continuity programs with my products through my coaching clients.

I also had a few people do my high ticket done–for-you sales funnel and mini product business with price points between $25k to $50k and up. I sold three of those packages, and it went really well. That book made me over $100K, and that was before I got serious about it.

Once I got serious about it, I started producing content on YouTube and optimizing the content to build a subscriber list. I always refer back to my book as the *free value incentive* for prospects to get on my list. That way, I keep relevant. I have followers on Facebook, YouTube, and my email list, plus they subscribe to all these things on my website.

I'm building that audience size with new people, which is setting things up so I can launch more books and do more things in the future.

How much have you made from your product business because of the book?

That $100k profit is not including what it did for my product business – that's just from coaching. My product business has tripled since the launch of my first book. I was doing close to $15k net when I started, and now I'm doing six figures in the last 30 days. In just product alone, it was over $50k in the last 30 days.

My product business is growing exponentially. In my opinion, you really have to have a book that gives you that authority status.

I selected the topic of the law of attraction because that was trending, and I didn't want to have to reinvent the wheel.

Now, I'm getting ready to launch my next book with you, *Ask Until It is Given*. I'm excited about it!

* * *

Looking at the four case studies above, we see that you can write a book to sell just about anything from vitamins and supplements, to software, to high-ticket coaching, to certifications, to board games, and more.

The next chapter is all about the **12 Profit Paths** you can create around your book to build a lucrative 6-figure business and beyond, just like the author-preneurs you just read about.

Chapter 2

12 Profit Paths to Unlock Your Book's 6-Figure Potential

Here comes the fun part!

In this chapter, you will learn about the different profit paths you can create on the backend of your book.

You saw how Mike Michalowicz, Brendon Burchard, Russell Brunson, and Matthew David Hurtado all built massively successful businesses using their books as lead magnets, income generators, and list-building tools.

Now it's your turn.

Here are 12 profit paths for your book to get started. Also, be sure to check out the **Bonus: 100 Ways to Make $100k** in the back of this book!

Just know there are endless ways to create income streams from your book, whether you are a non-fiction author or a fiction author.

Profit Path #1 – Digital Online Course/ Advanced Training Program Based on the Book

This is my favorite method because it is how I started my online business in 2005. I was teaching a class called *"How to Quit Your Job and Follow Your Dreams"* at Adult Education Centers, Community Colleges, Unity churches, and other local venues. One day, I realized I could reach a lot more people if I created a website and taught my course online.

Within my first 30 days, I made $2,500, and I was hooked on making money online! At the time, I was selling my ***Quit Your Job & Follow Your Dreams*** 6-week online course, and it was going really well.

It's important to know that you don't want to put *all* of your content in the book you write and publish; leave out some of the advanced material for your online course.

We'll talk more about that in the next chapter, where I discuss the three types of books you should be writing if you want to generate new income streams.

There are several ways to create a digital course and sell it online. Since I've had an online business for 16 years now, I'm going to give you three of the easiest ways:

1. If you have a website and blog with traffic, create a sales page and sell your course from your website. You can deliver it easily by sending PDFs or video links in an autoresponder sequence using email providers like

AWeber or mailchimp. This is the simplest and least technical way to start generating income.

2. If you don't have a website, you can easily create a course on platforms like Thinkific (this is what I use) or Teachable and sell it there.

3. Build a website on WordPress and install a membership plugin like Wishlist and put all your course material in the training site. Once someone signs up for your course, they will get a username and login and be able to access your course 24/7.

Many authors use the book as a starting point for their online courses and go deeper into the subject matter. Your book is the perfect outline for your online course!

You can't include everything in a book; there just isn't enough time or room. An online course is a great place to provide additional material that would make it very appealing to your prospects.

If desired, have different price points for the online course with various added benefits.

For example, you could add a private Facebook Group, Email Coaching, Group Coaching, or 1:1 Coaching and charge more.

Next up is…

Profit Path #2 – Paid Webinar Training

Sandi Krakowski, 7-Figure Entrepreneur, has made millions with social media, was teaching a 2-hour webinar several years ago for $47. I paid for and attended that webinar. Sandi had 500 spots open for the webinar and used paid advertising, her email list, and social media to drive traffic and register attendees. She sold all 500 spots and made a whopping $23,500.

If you did that four times per year, you would generate close to six figures in income just from eight hours of your time!

Of course, you would have to do some pre-work, like creating the webinar landing page and running paid ads, but the return on investment could be huge.

People love engaging with authors and being able to ask questions directly. Also, the low price point of $47 makes it affordable and accessible.

Profit Path #3 – Membership Site with Additional Content Dripped Monthly

I recently started following Carrie Green, the Founder and CEO of the Female Entrepreneur Association, and ran some numbers on her $37 per month membership site. It turns out she has over 4,500 members, which generates about $166,500 per month in revenue!

That's huge! Six figures per month from a $37 per month membership program! Unbelievable!

Don't think running a program like hers doesn't require a massive amount of work behind the scenes because it absolutely does. She likely has a huge team to support her efforts.

However, I wanted you to see the numbers behind a successful membership site like hers.

If your book and niche topic is something that you can continue to teach and build on, having a membership site makes sense and is also a great way to have *predictable paychecks*!

Profit Path #4 – Live Workshop or Seminar

I recently attended a 4-day event with Coach Christian Michelson in Ft. Lauderdale, Florida, and I watched him make four offers during the event and generate seven figures in income!

Christian is the author of a few different books and gives away tickets to his live events for those in his $199/month membership program. Let me clarify that he charges $99 for the event, but he returns the money to you in cash on Day 3 of the event to ensure people show up to it.

If you are selling a high-end mastermind or year-long program, inviting people to a 3-day event is a great way to get people to raise their hand.

Once prospects are at your event, you want to deliver valuable content, build the relationship, and then offer your high-ticket programs.

He sold $99 tickets to the event, refunded them to attendees on the third day, and then generated $1 million in sales at the event. There were probably 200+ people at the event.

Profit Path #5 – High-Ticket Retreat

I've seen week-long retreats selling for $25,000 to $30,000! People love to take luxury *working vacations* that they can also write off as a business expense.

Gina Devee of **Divine Living** has several different programs, such as her 12-month live course and her 90-day Elite Private Coaching. She also has week-long retreat to luxurious locations.

Carolin Soldo, another 7-figure income earner, offers a package that she calls her *"Powerhouse Coaching,"* and I believe it is the highest level she offers and sells for around $35,000.

People want transformation more than anything. Spending a week with someone who can guide them and hold their hand via coaching is a great way to achieve that.

If you are looking for a high-ticket product to sell on the backend of your book, consider creating a high-ticket weeklong retreat that others would love to attend.

Profit Path #6 – 8-12 Week High End Coaching or Consulting

I began my online business in 2005, selling online courses for $197. It wasn't until I created my own high-ticket programs ($10K-$35K+) that I started making six figures.

There are a couple of ways to do this.

You can enroll people in an 8-, 10-, or 12-week program and help them get results (transformation) during that time.

If students want to continue working with you, they can join your year-long coaching program for $1,000, $1,500 or $5,000+ per month or more.

I started my first private coaching program at $1000 per month and offered weekly calls and a private Facebook Group. One client = $12,000 in revenue. Not bad for an hour or two of work per week!

The first time I offered it, I filled it up!

Students will always be willing to pay big money to get big results.

If you don't like coaching, then I would recommend creating and selling an online digital course.

Profit Path #7 – Mastermind Group

A Mastermind Group is usually a 6-month or year-long program with the VIP or Elite group of your best clients.

Shanda Sumpter, founder of HeartCore Business and best-selling author of *Core Calling: How to Build a Business that Gives You a Freedom Lifestyle in 2 Years or Less* currently has a 10-million-dollar business with three main offerings. (She may have others, but these are the ones I know about.

- Pace Club – helping members build an email list and following. This is her foundational and starter program for $1,997. It is an information product with coaching.

- Her next offering is a yearlong mastermind group at $1,000 per month, consisting of two calls per month and a private Facebook group.

- She also has an advanced program called *The 1% Club*, and I'm not sure what the investment for that is. I think you must first be a client in the other programs to get invited to this one.

So, think about a mastermind program you can start based on the teachings in your book.

Profit Path #8- Certification

A Certification program is where you teach someone your methodology so they can train others. It's sort of like a "train the trainer" for what you do.

The *Profit First* certification and the *Pumpkin Plan* certification case studies I presented earlier in this book are great examples.

Mike created his own methodology, which he lays out in detail in his books, and then makes an offer. *"Hey if you want to teach this, then I'll certify you."*

It's a brilliant strategy because there is usually a large investment for someone to get certified.

A lady I know wrote a book on how she overcame fibromyalgia, and for $5,000, she certifies others as a "Fibromyalgia Coach."

She created the certification program because her time was limited, and she couldn't help everyone.

If your time is limited, a certification program is a great profit path for you.

Profit Path #9 - Licensing

Barbara Stanny, author of many bestselling books, including *Prince Charming Isn't Coming, Overcoming Underearning, Secrets of 6-Figure Women,* and *Sacred Success,* had a licensing program she called her "Business in a Box."

I'm not sure if she is still doing this, but in the past, you could license two of her programs (*Prince Charming Isn't Coming* and *Secrets of Successful High Earners*) for a yearly fee of $1,350, and then she would allow you to use all her materials.

Licensing is a great way to have others deliver your materials and get it out there for you. Obviously, you can't be everywhere all the time, so you could have licensees all over the world!

Profit Path #10 – VIP Day

Adding a VIP day on the back end of your book is a high-ticket path to high profits!

Sandi Krakowski charges $18,995 for her full-day VIP program. Here's the description of what she offers:

$18,995.00 for a full day with Sandi: "The day is held in our beautiful downtown Kansas City office. Full day is 5.5 hours in office (9:30-3:00 with lunch), 1-hour session a week before virtually and 1-hour session a week after, virtually. This is the most intensive way to bring results into your social media marketing quickly. You may bring one guest – an assistant or social media manager."

I'm not saying you have to charge $18K+ for your VIP Day. Start at a price point you are comfortable with or a little beyond your comfort zone if you want to challenge yourself. You can raise your prices as you get more VIP Day clients, testimonials, experience, and confidence.

Some Author-preneurs do a VIP Day virtually and charge anywhere between $997 and $9,997. Some do it face-to-face (like Sandi does) and charge $4,997 to $25,000+. Either way, the nice part is a VIP Day has a high-perceived value.

As marketing expert and bestselling author of *The Highly-Paid Expert*, Debbie Allen says:

*"Build value around offering more of your personal time. For example, you can include a pre-program questionnaire and a preview call to help your client get ready for their VIP day. Your program may also include a 30- to 60-day email follow-up before and/or after your VIP day, in order to clarify key points. This guarantees success for both the client and the expert. When you have an expert program that offers solutions, people will begin paying for your time right away. When you can take someone **farther and faster** to see immediate results, they will pay even more for your valuable time."*

VIP Days are a good option if you want to get a fast influx of cash in your business without a long-term coaching commitment.

Profit Path #11 – Done-For-You Service

Jennifer Spivak, also known as the *Facebook Ads girl*, has a Done-For-You Facebook ad service that she sells for $5000 a month with a 4-month minimum (at the time of the writing of this book) and includes the following:

"I'll create your campaigns, design your ads, set your targeting, and even place your pixels so you can breathe easy."

What can you sell as a Done-For-You service on the back end of your book?

Let's say your book is about starting a profitable blog. You could offer a Done-For-You "Set Up Your Blog" service for several hundred dollars and have more add-on features available.

Or, if you are a graphics designer with a book about branding, you could offer Done-For-You logos or branding packages.

Think of a Done-For-You service related to your book that readers would be willing to pay to have done.

If you don't have the skillset to deliver the services, you could partner with someone who does and create a revenue share.

People LOVE Done-For-You services and are willing to pay top dollar for them.

I know because I've done many Done-For-You services over the years, and they are very lucrative.

My previous business coach has someone who handles his Facebook ads (a Done-For-You service provider) for $5,000 per month.

I want to be clear that offering a Done-For-You service is *not passive income*, though. It requires top-notch skills and time. So, if that's not what you're looking for, consider creating a digital online course instead.

Profit Path #12 – Sell A Physical Product

Think about how much movie production companies make on the backend with products such as stuffed animals, tee shirts, mugs, hats, etc.

Is there a physical product that complements your book you could sell that readers would enjoy?

For example, essential oils are very popular right now. If you did a book on the health benefits of essential oils and sold products from your website, you would make money on those tangible products.

You could also create your own monthly "box" subscription service around your book. Let's say you write a book on dog training and then offer a monthly subscription for dog-training products to your readers.

You could also design a custom t-shirt around your book and sell that as well.

The possibilities are endless.

* * *

Fiction authors can also create programs, products, and services to sell on the backend of their books.

For example, my client, Dr. Jeffrey Donner, writes medical mystery and other types of novels. He has been a psychologist for over 30 years and includes a lot of psychological material in his book.

He is currently creating an online course on Emotional Intelligence. He said that the material in his online program would be equivalent to a year or more of therapy with him.

Think about the characters in your book and see if you can come up with a digital course, physical products, or something that goes with the *theme* of your book.

A great example of selling physical products for fiction books is the mega-hit book *50 Shades of Grey*. When I visited their website, I saw they were selling three products:

1. *50 Shades of Grey* Wine.

2. *50 Shades of Grey* Teddy Bear wearing a little black leather outfit and handcuffs.

3. *50 Shades of Grey* sexual toys collection.

Even if you are a fiction writer, you can absolutely sell on the backend of your book.

It looks to me like the *50 Shades of Grey* sales and marketing team (or the author) made affiliate arrangements with these other companies to share in the profits when a sale is made.

Start brainstorming on some ideas of profit paths you can create around your book.

Over the next week, I want you to contemplate this question:

What are at least three favorite ways to add new revenue streams to your book?

Chapter 3

Three Types of Income-Generating Books

Most authors aren't thinking about building a 6-figure business when they write their books (aside from dreaming of BIG royalty checks), so they write books that are *income-blocking* instead of *income-generating*.

In this chapter, I am going to teach you the three types of books to write when using the *Backwards Book Launch* method:

1. The What, but not the How Book

2. The Information Overload Book

3. The Hybrid Book

The What... But Not How Book

Giving the *what* but not the *how* is about teaching others *what* to do, but not *how* to do it.

For example, let's say I am going to write a book on *"How to Create a 6-Figure Automated Webinar Funnel"* to teach people how to drive traffic to their site with Facebook ads and sign-up prospects into high-ticket programs. (I taught this before in my private coaching program, so it's a good example to use.)

Instead of giving readers the detailed step-by-step instructions on how to set it up, I teach them only the "what" by introducing the concepts of funnels and high-ticket programs.

Here's what the steps would look like:

Step 1: Create a 45-minute webinar on your topic.

Step 2: Sign up with Stealth Webinar and have them set up your automated webinar for you.

Step 3: Create a new list in Aweber or another email service provider you use; this list is for your automated webinar attendees.

Step 4: Create follow-up autoresponders to go out daily to the webinar attendees.

Step 5: Create a landing page for people to sign up for your webinar.

Step 6: Provide that landing page link to Stealth so that they can re-create it.

Step 7: Include a link to your Stealth webinar landing page on your website.

Step 8: Set up a thank-you page for visitors who sign up for your automated webinar with a personal video from you.

Step 9: Create your Facebook ad to send people to a landing page to sign up for your webinar.

THREE TYPES OF INCOME-GENERATING BOOKS · 57

Step 10: Test various Facebook ads to get your winning ad.

Step 11: Set up scheduling software for prospects to schedule a time to talk to you about the webinar.

Step 12: Conduct strategy sessions to sign up people into your program.

Do you see how these steps are the "what" but not the "how"?

Of course, in this type of book, I would give examples and stories on each step, but I would NOT be teaching the details or the *how* for each step.

You will see this method often used for webinars. The reason experts teach only the *what* and not the *how* is because it's too time-consuming. You can't teach something that takes hours, days, or weeks to learn in a 1-hour webinar or a 100-page book.

The other reason ***not*** to teach the "what" is because if it is based on technology, then that information could become outdated quickly.

The truth is there is value to teaching people the steps to do something. I paid my coach a lot of money to learn how to set up my automated webinar funnels.

I want you to feel comfortable with this and know that you are not trying to trick people using your book by only giving them the *what* and not the *how*.

Obviously, a book can't teach everything in your brain on the subject (unless you want it to be a 300+ page book, and then people probably won't take the time to read it). People want fast information in easily digestible, bite-sized pieces. They no longer want or expect the manifesto.

It's your job to give them what they want – the information. If they need more clarification, they can sign up for one of your advanced programs to get that additional help.

Many people buy books that have only the "what" and figure out "how" to implement it on their own.

So, remember, in this type of book, you just tell them *what* to do, but not *how* to do it.

Reserve the *how* for your follow-up programs.

The next type of book you could write is…

The Information Overload Book

I remember being on a call with my Coach, Jason, and telling him that I was going to write a book teaching others how to become a #1 bestselling author.

Jason was very confused since I had a high-ticket Done-For-You program. He asked why I wanted to write a book on the topic since it was my "secret sauce" and how I was generating 6-figures in my business.

The answer to his first question about *why* write the book in the first place was that first and foremost, I am a writer, and I love to teach! I also felt it would be a great way to attract new clients into my (Done-For-You) Bestseller program as I would get a lot of exposure with my book.

My coach cautioned me, saying, *"Okay if you have to write this book, then there are only two ways to write it. One is to give the what, but not the how. And the other way is to give them every detail of what you do (making it so overwhelming) that they will be begging to hire you instead of doing it themselves!"*

It's funny he said that because in Case Study #4 above, when I asked my client, Matthew David Hurtado why he hired me, he said:

"It's time invested. Who has the time?

You didn't learn this stuff overnight, and you can't teach somebody how to do it overnight.

There's still going to have to put an ample amount of time to get to where you're at.

So, I'd rather just employ you to do what you do, and I'll just focus on being better at what I do."

People who have successful businesses value their time first and foremost. Many don't want you to teach them how to fish; they want to pay you to give them the fish!

That's why I created my Done-For-You programs. I have other less expensive programs available, like my online course based on my book "28 Books to $100K", but my Done-For-You services fill a need in the marketplace for busy entrepreneurs!

I really wanted to teach people exactly what I was doing so they could have the same success. Also, the reality was that I couldn't help everyone. I have very limited spaces in my Done-For-You programs.

So I ended up writing that book, *Bestseller in 30 Days*, and I gave readers everything I knew about getting books to the bestsellers list. My "information overload" strategy worked because many of the book's readers have hired me. They often tell me that they hired me because the information about the process was too overwhelming for them to do it themselves.

Publishing *Bestseller in 30 Days* has helped my business grow in multiple ways, such as new people learning about who I am; new subscribers to my email list; new potential clients for my Bestseller programs; new income generated; and new sales of my books on Amazon.

You might want to consider writing an *information overload* book because you can't help everyone in the world with your programs. For some of my programs, space is limited.

So, this type of book would allow you to share your knowledge with a lot of people while bringing new clients to your door.

Again, think about how many clients you can take into your programs. If you are selling Done-For-You services, how many clients can you realistically work with at the same time? If space is limited, then this is a good type of book to write.

If you can teach an unlimited amount of people, then write the *what but not the how book* instead.

Another reason to write an *information overload book* is because people don't usually realize how much work is actually involved in what you are teaching them.

I know that saying "Become a #1 Bestselling Author" sounds easy, but it's not. It takes a lot of work on the backend for us to create and publish a high-quality book and get that book to #1 on multiple bestsellers lists.

One of my Amazon Bestseller clients, Shellee Howard, came to me with no book title and no idea on what "type" of book to write. She felt her business needed a book to attract new clients, make more money, and elevate her authority so she could become the go-to expert in her industry.

We went back and forth between doing the *what but not the how book* OR the *information overload book*.

Shellee Howard is a college consultant with a business that helps families get their kids into the college of their dreams at the lowest tuition possible. The last time I checked, she charges over $5000 for her services, and her work is very labor-intensive.

After much discussion on which type of book she should do, Shellee decided to give away everything she knows on the subject and write the *information overload book*.

The 3 reasons for this decision were:

1. She can only take on a limited number of clients due to the labor-intensive nature of this type of work.

2. She really wanted to help families send their kids to college.

3. She knew that most people didn't realize all the work involved in getting the result she offers. She felt readers would quickly realize how much work and time is involved, and then they would hire her. Most people don't have the time, skills, energy, or desire to do it themselves.

I'm happy to say we published Shellee's book, *How to Send Your Student to College Without Losing Your Mind or Your Money*, and it's been on the bestsellers list ever since.

Shellee uses the book at networking events and book signings. It is a powerful lead magnet that constantly attracts new clients into her business.

Our strategy worked! I'm very proud of Shellee because she put her heart and soul into this book, and it's really paying off.

She is now considering starting a certification program.

The last type of book you could write is a hybrid of the above two types of books ...

The Hybrid

This type of book would be part *"what but not how"* and part *"information overload."*

Let's go back to the example above where I outlined the 12 steps on *"How to create a 6-Figure Automated Webinar Funnel"* and look at those 12 steps again:

Step 1: Create a 45-minute webinar on your topic.

Step 2: Sign up with Stealth Webinar and have them set up your automated webinar for you.

Step 3: Create a new list in Aweber or another email service provider you use; this list is for your automated webinar attendees.

Step 4: Create follow-up autoresponders to go out daily to the webinar attendees.

Step 5: Create a landing page for people to sign up for your webinar.

Step 6: Provide that landing page link to Stealth so that they can re-create it.

Step 7: Include a link to your Stealth webinar landing page on your website.

Step 8: Set up a thank-you page for visitors who sign up for your automated webinar with a personal video from you.

Step 9: Create your Facebook ad to send people to a landing page to sign up for your webinar.

Step 10: Test various Facebook ads to get your winning ad.

Step 11: Set up scheduling software for prospects to schedule a time to talk to you about the webinar.

Step 12: Conduct strategy sessions to sign up people into your program.

In this hybrid book, you would choose a few steps in the process and give the reader the *what* and the *how* on those steps only (all the details/information overload). So, I could pick the first three steps and give them the *what* and the *how*. For steps 4-12, I give them only the *what*. To get the rest of the *"how"* for steps 4-12, readers would have to sign up for my advanced training or coaching.

This type of book leads naturally to your follow-up programs.

Years ago, I was added to Jeff Walker's email list because he was promoting his *Product Launch Formula* program.

Jeff was using the "Sampler" method; he had four video trainings about his Product Launch Formula.

After the last video training, he made an offer for his *Product Launch Formula* program.

Of course, you could take what you already learned in the video training and try to do it on your own, OR you could sign up, pay the fee, and get the expert's help. This option would save you lots of time, energy, and money trying to figure out all the details on your own.

Jeff Walker only gave the "how" in those four training videos. To get the rest of the information, you would have to sign up for his paid program.

It really is a great method of teaching and works well when writing books to attract your ideal clients.

Income-Generating Books

These three types of books I mentioned above are all income-generating books and should get you thinking about a few profit paths for your book.

Once you know the profit path, that will help you decide which type of books you should write.

In this book you are reading; which method do you think I am using?

- The What But Not The How
- Information Overload
- The Hybrid

In this book, I'm using the *what but not the how method.*

The reason I chose this type of book is because I feel that just outlining the material is very valuable information and some readers can take this information and run with it.

Teaching exactly how to implement each of the 12 profit paths I outlined in this book would be extremely difficult without making the book 300+ pages.

So, I give the reader the "what," and they can implement it on their own. If they need help, then my Bestselling Author program is an option for anyone who wants to work directly with me.

You can apply to speak with me about creating a profit path for your book by visiting **bestsellingauthorprogram.com**, filling out the application, and scheduling a time to speak with me.

It makes more sense to give valuable information (the what) and then providing readers a way to reach out to me if they want my help implementing the information (the how).

When thinking about your book, what type do you think would be good to write based on the profit path(s) you selected for your book? Also, consider *why* this type of book is best to write.

- The What But Not The How
- Information Overload
- The Hybrid

Things to consider are:

How many clients can you take on for your backend programs? If this is a small number, consider writing the *information overload book*. If you can take on unlimited clients, I would do the *what but not the how book* or *the hybrid.*

Income-blocking books are long books that teach the *what* and the *how* leaving little opportunity for follow-up programs.

If you taught the *what* and the *how*, then your book would probably be 300 pages or more.

These three types of income-generating books outlined here are designed to lead your readers on a path to working with you on a deeper level and implement your teachings.

It's different for fiction authors because they are writing novels, but they can still sell products on the backend of their book if they think creatively. I shared the *50 Shades of Grey* and Dr. Jeffrey Donner's *Emotional Intelligence* examples in the last chapter.

Fiction authors can make money with products, speaking engagements, and other profit paths by creatively using their books to build a business.

Now it's time to use the 6-figure calculator and chart to see exactly how you can create six figures or more with your book.

Chapter 4

Profit Path Calculator

SHOW ME THE MONEY!

Pick one or two Profit Paths from the list below, set a price point, and create your new 6-figure Income Profit Path for your book:

- Digital Online Course/Training Program Based on the Book (You Can Charge Anywhere From $97 to $1997+ for Your Online Program)

- Paid Webinar Training (I Would Keep This Low-Ticket at $47 or $57)

- Membership Site with Additional Content Dripped Monthly ($27 or $37 a month to make this affordable)

- Live Workshop or Seminar (Charge anywhere from $99 to $2000 per ticket. If you are planning to upsell attendees at the event to your higher-priced program, offer this at a low cost).

- High Ticket Retreat (transformation is the name of the game here; what transformation can you offer at this event? How much is that worth to people? $5k? $10k? $25k? $35k or higher?)

- 8- to 12-Week High-End Coaching or Consulting ($3,000 to $10,000+ is a good price point)

- Mastermind Group ($1K to $5K+ per month)

- Certification ($5K to $10K+)

- Licensing ($1K - $3K+ Per Year)

- VIP Day ($997 to $25K+)

- Done-For-You Service ($5K to $25K+)

- Sell a Physical Product (prices vary)

> **Fill in the blanks below:**
>
> To make six figures from my book, my first path to profit is: _____. I will price that program at $_____ and I will sell _____ number of programs to generate six figures.

Example:

To make six figures from my book, my path to profit will be a digital online course priced at $997 and I will sell 101 of these courses to generate six figures with my book. 101 x $997 = $100,697!

You can add more than one profit path to your book.

You could offer a standalone digital product and upsell those buyers to a 12-week group coaching program for $5000.

Mix and match the profit paths and watch your income soar!

Below is a sample chart showing what creating multiple streams of income with your book can look like.

Program Type	Program Price	Number of Sales	Annual Income Generated
Digital Online Course	$297	350/year 29/month	$103,950
Paid Webinar	$57	500/quarter 2000/year	$116,000
Membership Site	$47/mo.	1000	$564,000
Live Event	$997	150	$149,550
Luxury Retreat	$25K	100	$250,000
8-12 Week Coaching Program	$5000	40/year	$200,000
Private Mastermind	$1000/mo.	120/year 10/month	$120,000
Certification	$5000	24/year 2/month	$120,000
Licensing	$1500	100/year	$150,000
VIP Day	$5000	200/year	$100,000
Done-For-You Service	$3000	48/year 4/month	$144,000
Physical Product	$100	1000	$100,000

Now, it's your turn to create your 6-7 figure Profit Path around your book.

Program Type	Program Price	Number of Sales	Annual Income Generated
Digital Online Course	$		$
Paid Webinar	$		$
Membership Site	$		$
Live Event	$		$
Luxury Retreat	$		$
8-12 Week Coaching Program	$		$
Private Mastermind	$		$
Certification	$		$
Licensing	$		$
VIP Day	$		$
Done-For-You Service	$		$
Physical Product	$		$

Wasn't that fun?

Starting with a digital product is the fastest and easiest way to start generating income around your book.

Once you create a digital course, then it's easier to add on other income streams.

For example, create a 6 to 8-week online course around your book or even a 4-week mini-course.

Don't try to give people everything in the course; just try to help them get a result.

Once your online course is up and running, add an 8-week group coaching program and charge $5000+ to join. The beauty of doing it in this order is that creating the online course forces you to create the content. Adding the high-ticket coaching is easy because you now have the curriculum for the students already set up, allowing you to add weekly group coaching calls.

Brilliant, right?

It's the perfect way to get started.

Then, you can stack these profit paths on top of each other and build a real empire!

Chapter 5

Why Writing Shorter Books are Better & They Have a Higher ROI

Because we live in a high-technology, fast-paced world, we are all very distracted, and our time is fragmented. Gone are the days when people would purchase a 300+ page book on a topic and block out leisurely reading time.

Now our time is broken up into very short and disjointed periods with continual interruptions such as email, text messages, Facebook, Twitter, LinkedIn and Instagram feeds, etc.

Consequently, people have diminished attention spans. They still want to learn new things; they just want to learn them quicker and faster.

Studies have shown that people want shorter books that they can consume in a few hours instead of longer books that they will most likely never finish.

For example, instead of writing a book on the A-Z of Marketing, it's better to write a series of books that focus on one topic. The series could include books on topics such as Writing Persuasive Sales Copy, Creating Facebook Ads, Building a Profitable Blog, How to Create an Automated Webinar, etc.).

So, think about your topic and then break it down into a series of books instead of only one book.

THINK MICRO INSTEAD OF MACRO TOPICS

There's a saying *"Niche and Grow Rich."*

How Keywords Can Help You Figure Out Your Audience and What Book to Write

Amazon is a crowded marketplace where readers find books using *keywords*. Readers enter the keywords that help them find the perfect book to solve their problem.

For example, the book that you are currently reading, **Backwards Book Launch: Reverse Engineer Your Book to Unlock its Hidden 6-Figure Potential,** is found with the following seven keywords that I researched and selected when publishing this book:

- ✓ Book Launch
- ✓ 6-Figure Author
- ✓ How to Market a Book
- ✓ Multiple Streams of Income
- ✓ Self-Publishing Books
- ✓ How to Make Money Writing
- ✓ How to Make a Living as a Writer

Figuring out your keywords (especially if you have not written your book yet) will help you get clarity on your topic. Then, you can research how people are searching for information on that particular topic on Amazon.

I often see my clients *guess* which keywords are best for their book, and 99% of the time, they have the *wrong* keywords.

The best way to find the right keywords is by doing a brain dump of what you think readers would enter in a search box to find books about your topic.

If they are, in fact, keywords that buyers are searching for, they will self-populate in the search bar on Amazon. If they don't pop up, you shouldn't use those keywords.

Another tip when you are selecting keywords is to use the title of a competitor's bestselling book for one or two keywords.

My last keyword listed above is *"How to Make a Living as a Writer,"* which is a book written by Joanna Penn that is currently on the bestsellers list. Now, my book will show up in the search results when people enter that keyword phrase.

Once you know your keywords, that will give you more insight and focus into who your ideal audience and reader is.

Keywords can also provide you with some ideas for what books to write. You could actually find keywords from Amazon's search bar and use that as the title of your book.

I use **Publisher Rocket** to do all of my keyword research.

Once you've done some research on the keyword search terms, you can get busy writing a short book on that topic.

10 Reasons Why Writing Shorter Books Is a Great Idea:

1. Time and attention are in short supply.

2. Writing short books is a lot easier than writing long books.

3. You can write short books quickly (it took me three days to write the bulk of this book.) I have tweaked and edited it, but I wrote most of it over a holiday weekend.

4. Volume Boosts Your Visibility (especially on Amazon), and you can attract repeat readers who will follow you.

5. Short books involve less risk.

6. Short books allow you to create a series of books that explore your favorite subjects in far greater depth than you could do in a single, longer book.

7. The data shows that most people don't get through the first couple of chapters of a book. With short books, there's a better chance people will read your book because they won't feel so overwhelmed by the number of pages in the book.

8. Amazon has a "Short Reads" category. Although you can't select this category when publishing on KDP, if your book meets the page number criteria, Amazon will place your book in that category, and your book will get more exposure.

9. You can price your eBook cheaper to get a higher number of sales. At low price points, people are more willing to purchase while searching. The low cost makes it a "no-brainer" decision.

10. You can niche and grow rich by writing short books that are in very narrow categories and do very well.

Return on Investment (ROI)

I have a book that is over 200 pages and took me two years to write that doesn't sell very well.

In 2020, I wrote a book a month for an entire year, and those short books outsell the longer book 10 to 1. You can read all the details in my book, **28 Books to $100K**.

You are more likely to write and finish a shorter book than a large book because writing large books (50,000 to 75,000-words) can be an overwhelming and daunting task.

When I decided to write a series of *shorter books* between 12,000 and 20,000 words, it was easier, faster, and I was more excited about the project.

Once I was clear on the title, subtitle, and chapters for this book (as well as my profit paths on the backend), I set aside the time to get the book done.

I dedicated four hours a day on Labor Day weekend to write this book. I got 80% of it written in three days by blocking out a large block of time to write!

TYPING IS A GREAT SKILL TO HAVE

For 17 years, I was a paralegal and a legal secretary (my first career), so I type pretty fast (close to 100 words per minute.) I can get a lot done on a book in a short period of time.

If you aren't a fast typist, there are alternatives. You can speak your book into an app on your phone like "Rev" and have it transcribed for $1 per minute of audio recording. Then, edit and clean up the transcript, and voila! You have a book!

After I finished writing the book, I had the cover made by a designer, and then I published it on Amazon Kindle Direct Publishing (KDP). Once the book was published and had at least five reviews, I did a 2-day book launch to #1 bestseller, which I'll talk about later.

Choosing to write short books allowed me to write a book a month for an entire year and create $3,300+ per month in passive income!

I know this might sound crazy to you, and I'm not suggesting you need to do the same thing. I LOVE to write, and I

LOVE to teach, and this is FUN for me! (I recognize that writing books is not "fun" for everyone, and if it's not fun for you, then you can either speak your book or hire a ghostwriter. My ghostwriting team writes books for several of my clients.)

If you write shorter books and add a profit path to the end of the book like I'm teaching you here, you'll get more books published in less time and make more money.

That sounds like a winning recipe to me!

The **Backwards Book Launch method** is about reverse engineering your book's profits FIRST, not LAST!

Some good questions to ask yourself for these shorter books are:

- What topic are you an expert on?
- What would you love to teach?
- Have you overcome an obstacle that others may need help with?
- Can you create a series of shorter books with this topic?
- Can you write at least three books for a box set or series?
- What profit path do you want to create to help readers implement what you are teaching?

- If you are a fiction writer, what products or programs match the theme of your book(s) that you can sell on the backend?

- How much do you want to make?

Chapter 6

Seven Questions to Ask Before You Write Your Book

You absolutely must know *who* will buy your book and *why* they will buy your book. Don't try to write a broad-topic book that will appeal to the masses.

The books that are doing well are either niche books or ones that solve a specific problem.

When deciding on the topic of your book and the title, here are seven questions you must answer:

1. **Who is your audience?** Many times, authors write books they wish they could have read when they started _____. For example, I wrote a book on how to start a 6-figure business. I wrote that book to my younger self (the person I was when I started my business over a decade ago and the things I wish I knew.) Think about exactly who would buy your book. Maybe you have a business, and you are writing this book to your ideal client. Try to be as narrow as possible when deciding for whom you are writing the book.

2. **What benefits will readers gain from your book?** Make a list of all the benefits readers will gain from reading your book. Don't be afraid to be bold when writing this

list. For example, in this book, *"The Backwards Book Launch: Reverse Engineer Your Book and Unlock It's HIDDEN 6-Figure Potential,"* the title sends the message that authors will learn how to make more money with their books by reverse-engineering the process.

3. **What are the top 3-5 benefits readers will gain by reading your book?** Think about the *pain* your reader is experiencing and why they are looking for your book. People are more inclined to buy their way out of something instead of into something. What is your ideal reader buying their way out of? Being broke? Sick? Single? You must be clear on how your book helps minimize or eliminate pain.

4. **Survey Titles for Your Book** – I recommend coming up with as many titles as you can for your book. At least 5-10 if possible. Then, create a survey using SurveyMonkey and find the top two titles. The survey results may even give you insight into your next book or help you create a subtitle. Often, the results will be close for one or two titles. I did a survey for this book to find the best title, and **Backwards Book Launch** was the winner… but a close second was *"The Lazy Author's Guide to a 6-Figure Income,"* so I'll probably write a follow-up book using that title one day!

5. **Use Benefits in Your Subtitle** – Sometimes, the title doesn't clearly say what the book is about, so make sure the subtitle does! It should tell people exactly what they will learn from your book and why they should read it.

6. **Be Bold and Grab the Reader's Attention with your Title and Subtitle** – Gone are the days where you can be "subtle" when coming up with titles. Don't be boring. Some of the best performing books on the market have outrageous titles! For example: *"The Subtle Art of Not Giving a F*ck"* by Mark Manson; *"Love Yourself Like Your Life Depends On It"* (the title isn't so outrageous, but the cover on the book is a silhouette of a man holding a gun to his head with a red heart on his chest and it definitely grabs people's attention); *"You are a Badass"* by Jen Sincero; *"Unlimited Memory"* by Kevin Horsley (big claim). You get the picture. Don't be subtle, shy, or low-key. It's a crowded world, and you've got to stand out!

7. **Add Keywords to Your Title If Possible** – You don't want to start with the keywords, but if you can get one or two of the top keywords for your niche in the title or subtitle, that will help you get more visibility on Amazon.

Knowing your audience is the key to your success.

When writing this book, I knew that it would appeal to people who have already written and published a book as well as those who want to write a book.

Both audiences can apply the strategies I've outlined to add six figures to their book by adding 1-12 income streams.

Chapter 7

Publishing Your Book the Right Way

Publishing Your Book the Right Way is Step 2 of the *Backwards Book Launch Method*. Once you know your profit path, then you can take this step.

In his book, *Perennial Seller,* author Ryan Holiday examines the works of artists and authors to uncover why their work endures and thrives.

At the end of the day, it boils down to this:

"Crappy products don't survive."

Ryan goes on to say that the better your product is, the better your marketing will be. The worse it is, the more time you will have to spend marketing, and the less effective every minute of that marketing. This is precisely why all the "pre-work" matters so much.

It's best to know and strategize beforehand what you are trying to accomplish with your book.

I work together with my clients to create high-quality books. I always tell my clients, "I don't decide what books will do well; the market decides."

Focusing on the "pre-work" that Ryan speaks about, knowing who you're writing the book to and why, is a good start.

The writing has to be good. I've found from doing over 250 book launches that even people with high IQs and many college degrees are not always good writers.

That's why I work with some top-notch ghostwriters to get books written for my clients.

Be honest with yourself. If you're not a writer, then can you hire a ghostwriter.

Once you have done the pre-work and outlined your strategy, listed your reasons for writing the book, and determined the benefits for the reader, then you must publish and launch a *quality* product, including:

- A professional cover
- Valuable content that solves a problem (for nonfiction)
- A professionally formatted and edited manuscript
- Selecting the correct keywords and categories so the right people can find your book
- Writing a great book description that sells your book
- Having as many 5-star reviews as possible before you launch the book (minimum of 5)

Once you have a solid foundation and publish your book the right way on Amazon Kindle Direct Publishing (KDP), then you can do a proper "book launch" to get your book out into the world and on to the bestsellers list.

That is Step 3, which is outlined in the next chapter.

Chapter 8

Launching Your Book as a Bestseller

When Hollywood is getting ready to release a new movie, they start promoting it with movie trailers, ads, commercials, pre-showings, and more.

A book launch is very similar. Start spreading the word before you do a proper "book launch," which I will explain here.

The key to getting on a bestsellers list is having a high number of downloads in a short amount of time.

In my Bestselling Author program, I do a two-day massive book launch for my clients' books and get their books to #1 on the Bestsellers List on Amazon. (I also have programs where I launch books to the Wall Street Journal and USA Today Bestsellers lists).

Before I do this, I spend 10-12 weeks getting the book and all the moving parts ready for the book launch.

When everything is set up and the book is published on Amazon with great reviews, I follow these steps:

- **Hire Several Book Promoters** to promote the book on scheduled days of launch. I either do a 2-day free launch of the eBook or a 1-day paid launch with the eBook priced at $0.99.
- **Set up automated posts on social media** (Twitter, Facebook, Facebook groups, LinkedIn, and Instagram)
- **Send out an email about the promotion** to my email list that I've been building for 10+ years.
- **Capture screenshots of the book on the bestsellers list.**
- **Create a marketing collage** and start promoting it as a bestseller once we get to the bestsellers list.
- **Set up media interviews** for my client once we get to the #1 bestsellers list.
- **Set up Amazon Ads**

I am frequently asked, "How many books do you have to sell to get to a bestsellers list?"

Amazon updates their bestsellers lists a few times a day, so it depends on the competition in the categories you selected on the day of the launch.

To get your book to #1 in a category, you must beat the sales ranking of current the #1 book in that category on launch day. It's a numbers game.

I've done book launches that had between 500-4000 downloads in 1-2 days. And I am happy to say I have 100% success getting my clients' books to hit #1 on multiple Bestseller's List.

Sometimes it takes a few hundred sales to get to the #1 Bestseller's List, or it could require a lot more for a highly competitive bestsellers list.

I can't teach all the details about categories, keywords, launches, and bestsellers list in this book because that is beyond its scope.

The goal of this book is to teach you how to build a 6-figure business on the backend of your book and make money as an author.

In the next chapter, I provide a book launch checklist and describe some of the activities involved in a proper launch.

Chapter 9

Backwards Book Launch Checklist

I like to break down my book launches into three phases: *Pre-Launch, Launch,* and *Post-Launch.*

Use this checklist to ensure you are prepared for a successful book launch.

PRE-LAUNCH

- Research your keywords and be sure to use them, if possible, in your title, subtitle, and book description (keywords are the words or phrases readers type in the search bar on Amazon to find your book and similar books).

- 30 days before your launch, post updates on social media about your upcoming book (warm up the audience); write a blog post if you have a blog.

- Decide on 5-10 titles for your book and do a survey using SurveyMonkey.

- Have 2-3 book covers made and post them on social media, asking people to vote for their favorite.

- Decide on a FREE gift to give away with your book to help build your email list and create a landing page. Or send them to your home page to sign up.

- Upload your book 1-3 weeks before the launch so you can get at least five reviews (the more, the better) before the promotion starts. Don't upload your book too far in advance of your launch because your book will only be included on Amazon's **"Hot New Releases"** list for 30 days after it is published. It is great for your book to be featured on this list.

- Once your book is uploaded and approved, start working on getting five reviews.

- Reach out to influencers (press, bloggers, or podcasters) and ask them to promote your book.

- Send a PDF copy of your book to influencers for reviews.

- Create a Facebook event and let friends and friends of friends know about your book launch.

- Write emails to send out to all your contacts and email list during launch week.

- If you are doing a video trailer, include your free dates or discounted dates for the launch and post it on YouTube two to four weeks before the launch to promote it.

- Upload your book to Amazon KDP and select two DIFFERENT categories.

- Research additional categories and submit to Amazon via a customer support ticket. Although you can only select two categories when uploading your book, Amazon permits you to include up to 10 categories. Ensure you select relevant categories that are not too competitive, so you can rank high on the bestsellers lists.

- Enter your seven keywords based on your research when publishing on Amazon KDP.

- Decide on launch date(s) and either make the book available for free or price it at $.99.

- Submit your book to the book promotion sites 1-2 weeks before your launch starts.

- If you are doing press releases, submit your press releases or find someone on Fiverr.com to submit your press releases to PR sites.

- Purchase a sponsored Facebook post and show it to friends of friends to get some exposure. Do this over three days.

- Go to Fiverr.com and buy some gigs from providers who will tweet your book to hundreds of thousands of people or post it on Facebook.

LAUNCH

- After the pre-launch period, it's time to capture everything and promote your book even more.

- Check your rankings on Amazon and take screenshots when you hit the Bestsellers Lists.

- You will also be on additional bestseller lists that Amazon doesn't show on your product page, so you have to find your book in all the categories you selected manually. Amazon only shows three bestseller lists on your product page (be sure to check international bestseller lists).

- Create a marketing collage and promote on social media once you are a bestseller!

POST-LAUNCH

- Continue to market your book once you are a #1 Bestselling Author; this is not a one-and-done event.

- Immediately set up Amazon Ads after the launch.

- Add the bestseller logo to your cover and resubmit to Amazon.

- Immediately set up media and podcast interviews once you become a bestselling author.

- Ask for reviews of your book from people who downloaded your book, especially if you did a free launch.

- When you have at least 20 reviews, and your book is on a bestsellers list, do a paid promotion with Bookbub.com. BookBub is the largest book promoter on the Internet! They have over 4 million subscribers and can guarantee sales of your book. One of my client's got over 31,000 downloads of her book based on one BookBub promotion.

- Add links to your bestselling book on the home page of your website (if you have one.)

- Include something about your book in your autoresponder series so that you are constantly marketing your book to your list.

Once you become a bestselling author, you hold that title for life. Ensure your cover reflects that, and include it on your social media sites, website, etc.

My books sell about 800+ copies per month (combined total), and if 5% of those readers sign up for my done-for-you program or my online course, that equals multiple six figures in income.

Getting your book on the bestsellers list and keeping it there is paramount to gaining new clients from your book. The fact is, if you are not on a bestsellers list, your book is invisible on Amazon.

Chapter 10

100 Ways to Make $100K

I created this list for both authors and coaches, consultants, speakers, healers, or entrepreneurs who wants to create multiple streams of income.

See below…

"100 Ways to Make $100K" should get your mind thinking of new ways to add multiple streams of income to your business:

1. **Digital Online Course (6, 8 or 10 Weeks)**
2. **Mini Online Course (4 Weeks or Less)**
3. **Masterclass**
4. **Live Course (Not Pre-Recorded)**
5. **Joint Venture Online Course Taught with Another Instructor**
6. **Membership Site**
7. **1:1 Coaching**
8. **Group Coaching**
9. **Done-With-You Coaching**
10. **Done-For-You Coaching**
11. **Do It Yourself**
12. **Paid Webinar**
13. **Watch Me Do It Live**
14. **Watch With Me Recorded**
15. **Power Hour**
16. **Live Workshop or Seminar**
17. **High Ticket Retreat**

18. High Ticket Coaching or Consulting

19. Mastermind Group

20. VIP Half Day

21. VIP Full Day

22. VIP In Person (1-Day)

23. VIP In Person (2-Day)

24. Speaking at Events

25. Keynote Speech

26. Certification Program

27. Licensing Intellectual Property

28. Business in a Box

29. Done-For-You Service

30. Done-With-You Service

31. Physical Products

32. Monthly Box Service

33. Private Label Service

34. Software

35. Private Label Product

36. Livestreaming Event

37. **Sell Affiliate Products**

38. **Sponsorships**

39. **Crowdfunding**

40. **Sell Technical Services such as Virtual Services, SEO services, website design, etc.**

41. **Selling Ad Space on Your Website**

42. **Sponsored Reviews**

43. **Network Affiliate Marketing**

44. **Sell Related Products to your book**

45. **Online Consulting**

46. **Develop an App.**

47. **Translation Services**

48. **Online Magazine or Newspaper**

49. **Podcasting with Sponsors**

50. **Radio Show with Sponsors**

51. **Sell Music**

52. **Sell Your Own Merchandise You Create**

53. **Paid Tweeting**

54. **Sell Stock Photography**

55. **E-Commerce Site**

56. Email Coaching
57. Pay Per Click
58. Pay Per View
59. Pay Per Project
60. Custom Painting
61. Arts and Crafts
62. Customized Readings
63. Sell Skills on Fiverr
64. Tech Support
65. YouTube Videos on Your Topic with Ads
66. Freelance Writing
67. Ghostwriting
68. Developing Online Courses for Others (Curriculum)
69. Sell a Game That You Create (Like *Rich Dad Poor Dad*)
70. CDs
71. DVDs
72. Home Study Program
73. Sell Food Products (yours or others)
74. Sell Food Services (yours or others)

75. **Sell Menu Plans**

76. **Tutor Kids**

77. **Write Slogans**

78. **Write Manuals**

79. **Bookkeeping Services**

80. **Accounting Services**

81. **Provide Customer Service**

82. **Relationship Advice**

83. **Virtual Assistant Services**

84. **Peer-to-Peer Lending**

85. **Compilation Book – Have Multiple People Pay to Write a Chapter in a Book That You Publish**

86. **Editing and Proofreading Services**

87. **Social Media Management Services**

88. **Personal Training Services**

89. **Sell Physical Products on Amazon**

90. **Hold Event and Sell Sponsorships**

91. **Grant Writing Services**

92. **Security Services**

93. **Nutrition Plans**

94. Virtual In-Home Coaching (Design, Feng Shui, or Organization)

95. Live In-Home Design Services, Coaching, or Consulting

96. Animal Training or Consulting

97. Chef Services

98. Travel Agent Services

99. Genealogy Services or Consulting

100. Create an Agency (Facebook Ad agency, Child Care, Nannies, Virtual Assistants, etc.)

Final Words

Most people don't have the desire, time, or skill set to do these types of book launches, which is why they hire and work with me.

I use a system that I've been developing since 2013 when I first launched my Bestselling Author program. I'm proud and happy to say that I also have an amazing team that works with me putting together these #1 bestseller Done-For-You book launches.

If it's your dream to be a #1 bestselling author and to make money from your book, visit bestsellingauthorprogram.com to set up a time to speak with me.

I love talking to author-preneurs!

Also, I don't want you to think that you won't make any money from your book royalties.

I have several clients that make $1000-$8000+ per month in royalties from their books, but that takes time.

I have another client whose book had over 1000 sales within three months of launching her book.

You can make money from royalties, but it can take time and usually requires that you publish more than one book.

No one has a crystal ball that tells you if your book will take off or not. All you can do is put out a quality book, do a proper book launch, keep your book on the bestsellers list, and then write more books if you feel inclined.

The best strategy to make money is to write books from which you can build multiple income streams on the backend.

By doing this, you increase your reach and impact with readers. It's a win/win!

I hope you've enjoyed reading this book! I enjoyed writing it for you.

I would greatly appreciate your honest review of this book on Amazon. To write a glowing review, visit

https://www.amazon.com/Michelle-Kulp/e/B006D4EQIY/!

Getting reviews is not so easy, but they help the author immensely!

So, if you could find it in your heart to write a review, I will be eternally grateful!

Here's to ALL of your Dreams Coming True!

About The Author

Michelle Kulp left a 17-year career in the legal field to follow her dreams of writing, teaching, and speaking. She started her first website, www.becomea6figurewoman.com, in 2005 to inspire women to live their passions, follow their dreams, and make 6 figures doing what they love!

Since 2013, Michelle has been helping authors write, publish and launch books to the Amazon, Wall Street Journal, and USA Today bestsellers list. To date, she's helped over 250 authors become #1 bestsellers. Michelle has written and published over 20 bestselling books.

You can connect with Michelle at:
www.bestsellingauthorprogram.com

Social Media

Facebook
Facebook.com/michelle.bachteler.kulp/

Facebook group/page:
Facebook.com/groups/28BooksTo100K

LinkedIn
LinkedIn.com/in/michelle-kulp-732b8615/

Twitter
Twitter.com/6figurewoman

Instagram
Instagram.com/michelle.kulp

28 BOOKS TO $100K

A Guide for Ambitious Authors Who Want to Skyrocket their Passive Income by Writing a Book a Month

MICHELLE KULP

FREE GIFT FOR MY READERS

I have a special gift for my readers! If you are serious about making a living as a writer, and maybe even writing a book a month so you can retire early…I have created a *Quick-Start Writing Kit* that is yours FREE for a limited time. This kit includes:

- 16 Rapid Writing Secrets
- Bestseller Checklist
- Annual Publishing Chart
- Income Tracker
- Book Creation Outline Template
- Author Archetype Assessment
- Video Training

Sign up NOW to receive your Quick-Start Kit at:
BestsellingAuthorProgram.com/free-module-28-days-to-100k/

Introduction

It's always been my dream to make a living as a full-time writer. Perhaps it's your dream, too.

In 2019, I read a blog post by Written Word Media[1] that said the average self-published author who makes $100K has 28 books published. I immediately thought, "I need to make a $100K with my books! I'm going to write a book a month and create a 6-figure passive income stream SOLELY from my royalties."

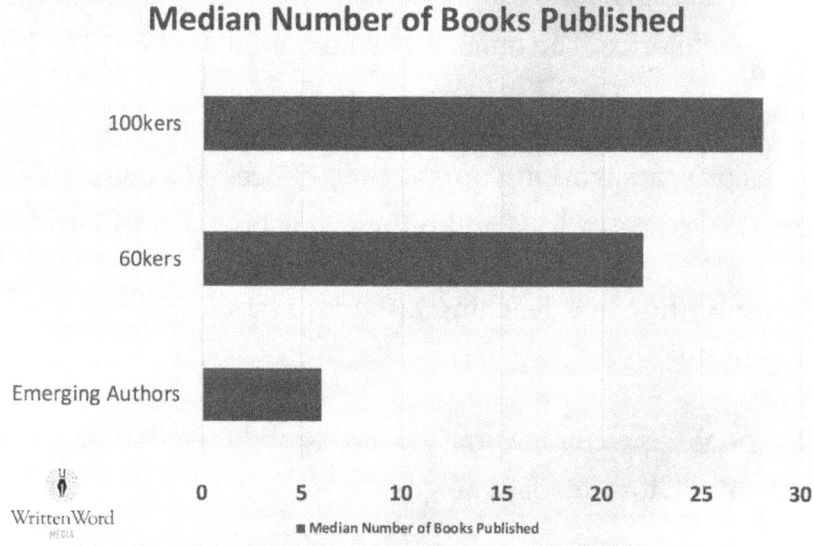

---

[1] https://www.writtenwordmedia.com/author-income-how-to-make-a-living-from-your-writing/

At the time, I had published eight books since 2011, but most of them were old, the information was outdated, and I had not been marketing them, so they died a slow death.

Starting in 2018, I spent more than a year writing the second edition of my book, "Quit Your Job and Follow Your Dreams." I was earning a few hundred dollars per month from this book but considering the amount of time I invested in writing, editing, publishing, and launching this *one* book, the payoff wasn't huge.

Seth Godin, who has published dozens of business books on sales and marketing, said, "One of my books took more than a year to write, ten hours a day. Another took three weeks. Both sell for the same price. The quicker one outsold the other 20 to 1."

When I read that quote, I realized I didn't need to spend months or years working on one book. I needed to write short books (100 pages or less) and publish one book per month.

Since writing and teaching are my passion, I knew I could easily do this!

My books, on average, are 100 pages, and they fit nicely into Amazon's "Short Reads" category.

> ‹ Kindle Store
>
> **Kindle Short Reads**
>
> 15 minutes (1-11 pages)
>
> 30 minutes (12-21 pages)
>
> 45 minutes (22-32 pages)
>
> One hour (33-43 pages)
>
> 90 minutes (44-64 pages)
>
> Two hours or more (65-100 pages)

I have focused mainly on nonfiction books.

I'm happy to tell you that after 12 consecutive months of writing a book a month, I was able to create $3,300 in monthly royalties!

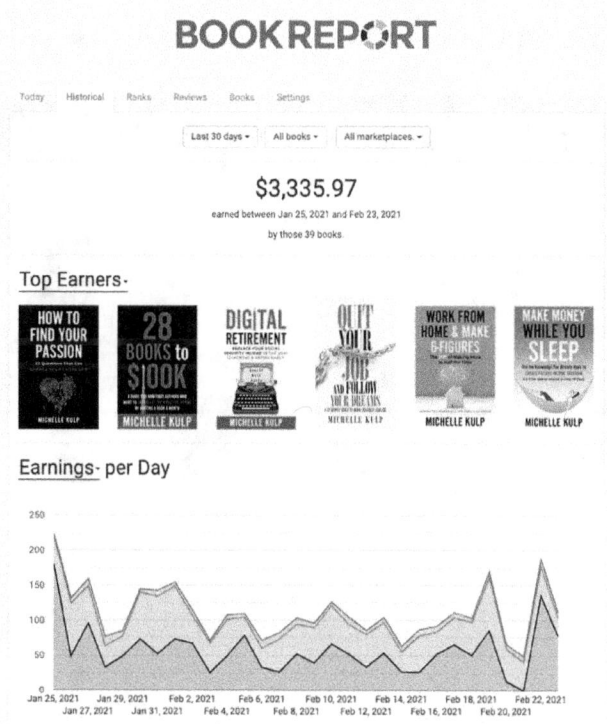

When I first publish a book, it brings in about $200-$300+ per month in royalties, and that amount increases over time and with each new book I publish.

I heard another author say, "Nothing sells your first book better than your second book." I've also found this to be true. In each new book I release, I include references to my previously published titles, which creates new readers for those books.

As I am writing these words now, I currently have 11 books on the Amazon Best Sellers list in the "Women & Business" category! My goal is to dominate this category (and other categories):

Here are some screenshots of those 11 books:

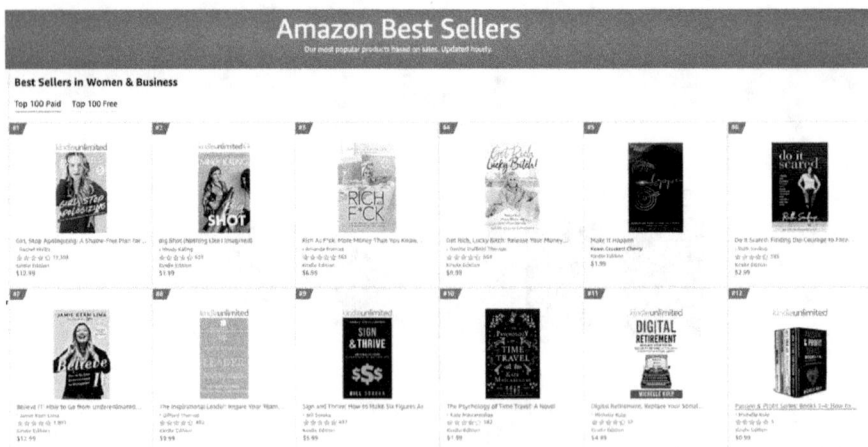

INTRODUCTION · 121

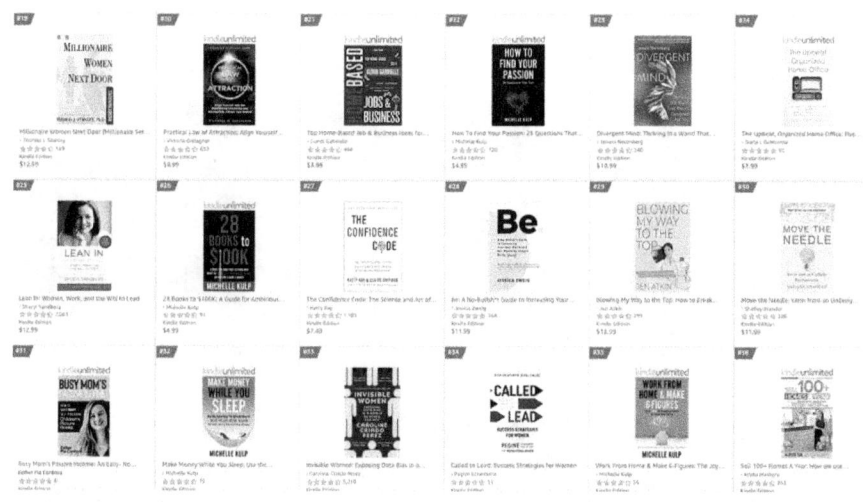

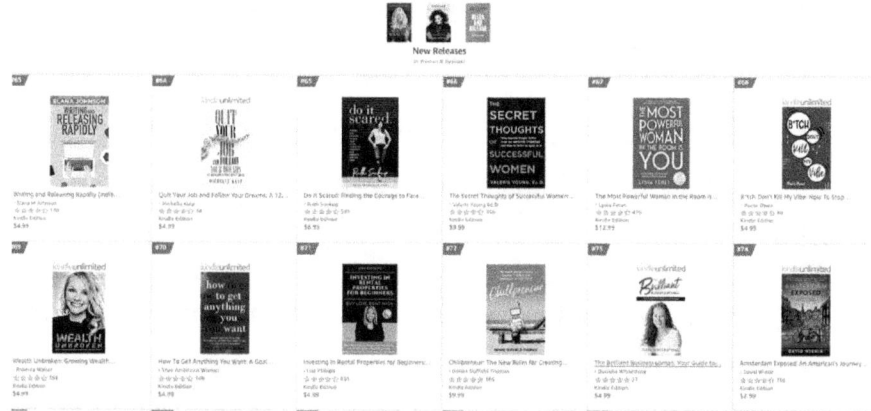

Volume Boosts Visibility!

I write books mainly in the business genre – books for entrepreneurs and authors; I've also written a few self-help books for women. We'll talk more about whether you should write in one genre only or diversify.

I decided to write this book for ambitious authors and entrepreneurs who have a desire to write quality books that serve readers AND want to earn a full-time income with their books. That is my goal as well.

Since January 2013, I have helped over 250 authors become #1 bestselling authors in my done-for-you program, www.BestSellingAuthorProgram.com.

Many of my business authors are making six or seven figures from speaking, coaching, consulting, etc. as a result of publishing books.

However, I do not have any students making six figures from publishing *just one book.*

If you're a business owner or an entrepreneur, it's smart to write a book that creates back-end income in the 6- to 7-figure range. I've used this strategy myself. I wrote an entire book about how to build the profit into your book first, before you write it. That book is: "Backwards Book Launch: Reverse Engineer Your Book and Unlock Its Hidden 6-Figure Potential."

Writing one book is great IF you have a plan to monetize that book (which is what I teach my clients). However, if you want to make passive income SOLELY from royalties, then *writing a book a month* can help you reach that goal if you're committed to doing the work.

You're probably thinking *"Michelle, this plan sounds like I would need to invest a lot of time in order to reach $100K a year."*

Yes, that's true. It will take you two years and four months to have 28 books published if you are publishing one book per month. However, I have learned from my good friend and multiple bestselling author Marc Reklau (who just this month earned over $20K from royalties on his books) that you don't need 28 individual books published on Amazon; you just need 28 "products" on Amazon. A product can be an audio book, or a box set in which you bundle two or more titles together and sell them as one product for a higher price. In addition to creating box sets from his books in the same genre, Marc also creates audio books to sell as a separate product. He also sells his books in other countries and in other languages on the Amazon platform.

BAM!

I'm writing a book a month and in this month's book, I'm sharing with you the process I have developed, what I've learned, and best practices.

When I tell my clients and other entrepreneurs that *I'm writing a book a month*, I get responses like, "I want to do that!", "Can you teach me how?", "Sign me up!" Because of the positive response, I have created an online course to go along with my **Book-A-Month** (BAM) system which also includes the training, templates, and checklists.

"28 Books to $100K" is for anyone who loves writing and wants to make a living as a writer. I know some authors who would love to quit their full-time jobs, which is a great motivator!

I can't guarantee your results because there are many variables. But I believe if you write a quality book each month on a topic that is in demand and you are consistent with your writing and publishing, then you will have success. I've set income goals for myself from writing a book a month, and so far I have reached those goals each month. I'll share my results with you soon.

Determine your goals and start there. Maybe you just want to write enough books to pay your cable bill, or maybe your mortgage payment or even ALL of your living expenses. The sky is the limit if you're willing to work for it!

Whatever your personal goal is… I believe that writing a quality "Book a Month" can help you increase your passive income and achieve your goals.

There's a lot to learn, so let's get started…

Chapter 1

Why Shorter is Better

"One of my books took more than a year to write, ten hours a day. Another took three weeks. Both sell for the same price. The quicker one outsold the other 20 to 1.

A $200 bottle of wine costs almost exactly as much to make as a $35 bottle of wine.

The cost of something is largely irrelevant, people are paying attention to its value.

Your customers don't care what it took for you to make something. They care about what it does for them."

~Seth Godin, Multiple Bestselling Business Author

In the past, big publishing houses could charge more for longer books. There was also a high demand from consumers who wanted to read longer books.

However, times have changed, and people now have less time and decreased attention spans.

Readers want short books!

Top 10 Reasons to Write Short Reads Books

1. Time and attention are in short supply, so there is a greater demand from readers for quick reads.

2. Writing short books focused on one topic is easier than writing a long book with multiple topics.

3. Fewer words require less time to write (it took me three days to write the bulk of this book.)

4. Volume Boosts Visibility (especially on Amazon). You can attract repeat readers who will follow you.

5. Short books involve less risk. Because you are not investing a considerable amount of time or money in creating these books, less than expected sales will not greatly impact you. In fact, you will learn what works and what doesn't work and then use that knowledge when writing more books.

6. You can create a series of short books that explore your favorite subjects in greater depth than you could do in a single, larger book.

7. In this article[2], much of the data shows that people do not finish reading books. Since shorter books

---

[2] https://www.theifod.com/how-many-people-finish-books/

require less time to read, there is a greater chance people will actually read your entire book.

8. Amazon has a specific category for these books called "Short Reads." You can't select this category when publishing on KDP, but if the number of pages in your book matches the criteria in that Short Reads category, Amazon will include your book in that category giving it more exposure.

9. You can set a lower price your eBook and get a higher quantity of sales.

10. You can *niche and grow rich* by writing short books in very narrow categories and do extremely well.

I love writing shorter books!

I spent a year writing the second edition of my book, "Quit Your Job and Follow Your Dreams," which ended up being 250 pages!

When I decided to do this "book a month" experiment, I wrote "How to Find Your Passion: 23 Questions that Can Change Your Entire Life" in about three weeks. I published it within 30 days, and right now, this is my top income generating book. It outsells "Quit Your Job and Follow Your Dreams" 10 to 1. I believe it's because people want shorter books with action items they can use to get quick results.

Of course, some books will do better than others. You never know what topic will appeal best to readers. The market decides what they like and don't like. All you can do is write the best book possible, do your research, launch like a pro, and then move on to the next one.

We live in a high-tech, fast-paced world. Most of us are extremely distracted and our time is fragmented. Gone are the days when people buy a manifesto type book and block out their entire weekend to leisurely read.

These days, our time is broken up into short and often disjointed periods. We face constant interruptions from emails, texts, phone calls, Facebook, Twitter, Instagram, and more.

Consequently, attention spans have diminished. The desire to learn new things exists but most people want to learn faster.

Consider this when writing books. Instead of writing a book on the A-Z of Marketing, write a series of short books that each focus on one narrow topic. For example, the series could include books on these topics:

- Writing Persuasive Sales copy
- Creating Facebook Ads
- Building a Profitable Blog
- How to Create a Webinar

Think micro-topics instead of macro-topics.

6 Types of Easy-to-Write Short Books

1. List or tip book
2. Step-by-step guide
3. Q&A interview focused on a specific topic
4. Single-question deep dive
5. Collection book (for example, top strategies, top recipes, or top performers in an industry)
6. Extended blog post – if you have a popular blog post, expand on it, and publish it as a short book

Return on Investment (ROI)

I've written long books and short books, and shorter books provide a better return on investment in my opinion.

I believe writing shorter books saves you time while increasing your revenue. For example, let's say you spend one full year writing a book (like I and many of my clients have done), and you earn $200 a month from that one book. If you were writing a book a month, you could have written 12 books, each earning $200 a month, and your income would be $2,400 per month or more instead of $200 per month!

BAM!

Moreover, you are more likely to finish writing and publish a shorter book because writing a large book that is 50,000 to 100,000 words can be a daunting task.

I work with clients who have spent years working on their "one book."

I encourage you to write short books. You can write the book in about two weeks and the editing process is much shorter.

When I send my final manuscript to my editor (I recommend always using a professional editor), she reviews it and sends it back to me with changes marked in the document. I review her suggested changes and accept or reject them. Then, I wait a day or two and read the book word for word (which is easy to do with a short book), and I always find a few typos and some changes I want to make.

A 250+ page book would require too much time to write, edit, and review, and I would not be able to publish a book a month with that many pages.

So, keep it short and save yourself the overwhelm! Readers want short books!

Chapter 2

Titles, Titles, Everywhere

If you are going to write a book a month, I suggest you have a designated notebook labeled, "Titles" or create a document on your *Notes* app on your smartphone or computer and keep adding to it. Just about every day, I read or hear something, and I think, "OMG, what a great title!"

Authors cannot copyright a title. So, the title for your book can be the same as another book that has been previously published. However, I would encourage you to slightly change the title and not copy a great title word-for-word.

For example, several writers contributed to a multi-author book called "Write and Grow Rich" which is similar to the classic book "Think and Grow Rich" by Napoleon Hill.

I talk more about different ways to come up with titles in the *Bestseller Checklist* chapter, but here are 50 fill-in-the-blank templates you can use as a launching point to create your amazing book titles!

Numbers Titles

1. [Number] Secrets to [do anything you're an expert at teaching]
2. [Number] Best Ways to Get Your [Book/Product] Done Fast
3. [Number] Strategies for More Productive [Activity]
4. [Number] Ways to [Result]
5. [Number] Quick & Clever [Subject you're an expert at] Techniques
6. [Number] Ways to [Boost/Enhance] Your [Career/Weight Loss/Dating Options] in [Number] Minutes a Day
7. [Number] Best [Resource(s)] for [Target Audience]
8. [Number] Steps to Better [Writing/Weddings/ Activity]
9. [Number] Secrets of Super Simple [Activity]
10. [Number] Best [Subject you're an expert at] Tricks You Haven't Tried
11. [Number] Unforgettable [People/Places/Subject]
12. [Number] Secrets to [Staying Slim/Making Money]
13. [Number] [Delicious/Trendy/Fast/Adjective] [Noun] You Will Love
14. [Number] Strategies to [do anything you're an expert at teaching]

15. Your Way to Real [Wealth/Health/Prestige/Result]

16. [Number] Tough [Subject you're an expert at] Questions and the Right Answers

17. The Mistake that Will Cost You [Number] [Dollars/Hours/Measurable cost]

How-to Titles

1. How [Current Event News] is/are Changing the [Economy/Industry]

2. The Best Way to [do anything you're an expert at teaching]

3. Your Guide to [Opportunities/to do anything you're an expert at teaching] that Pay(s) Off BIG

4. How to Win Free [Resource/Prize] to [Result]

5. Put Your Skills to Work to [Support/Follow/Achieve] Your [Dream, Goal, Plan]

6. How to Get a Dream [Career] [subject you're an expert at] Made Simple

7. How to Win at [Activity/Career]

8. [Subject you're an expert at] Made Easy

9. [Subject you're an expert at] in [Number] Simple Steps

10. How to Spot Bad [Subject you're an expert at] Advice

11. How to Cut Your Risk of [Problem]

12. Your Final Solution to [Problem]

13. More [Result], Less [Problem] — Here's How

14. How to [Result] and Not Get Burned

15. Easy [Subject you're an expert at] Secrets

16. Why You Shouldn't Ignore [Problem]

Benefit-Driven Titles

1. What Every [Writer/Plumber/Occupation] Needs to Know About [Your Expertise]

2. Why Someone Else's [Product] Could be Your [Chance/Result]

3. Save Hundreds of Dollars on [Activity/Item]

4. Avoid [Mistake]

5. Prevent [Consequence] by [Your Solution]

6. Celebrate [Result] through [Problem]

7. Stop [Mistake] Here's Why

8. Your Perfect [Result] Starts Now

9. Have More [Result]

10. Top Secret: How You Can Achieve [Result]

11. Got [Problem]? Here's How to [Result]

12. The [Result] You Can Get at [Home/Work/Place]

13. Supersize Your [Result]

14. Secrets of [Benefit Adjective] People

15. Smart People [Result]

16. Low [Risk/Cost/Problem], Big Results

17. A Surprisingly Simple Cure for [Problem]

These fill-in-the-blank templates will make it much easier for you to come up with titles.

PRO TIP: Use this same method for your chapter titles. Don't give away the whole book in your table of contents. You want to evoke curiosity, so people actually purchase your book. Create intriguing chapter titles that make people want to buy the book to learn more.

If you get stuck, look at titles on the bestsellers list in your genre for more ideas.

Looking at books that are successful and doing well will inspire and motivate you!

I use a program called "KDSpy" that allows me to see how many copies of a book are sold per month. This is invaluable information when you're deciding which books you want to write each month. When you see a successful book on Amazon, the next step would be to read the reviews and think about how you can write a better, different, or improved book.

It's important that you keep writing your book each month and stay on your timeline, even if you are not 100% sure what the final title will be. Just use a "working title" that can be changed when you're done writing.

Many times, I create the subtitle after I write a book because you learn things as you're writing, and the writing informs the title as well as the subtitle.

Use the fill-in-the-blank template below to plan out your 12-month book writing plan and get started now. Action is everything.

You can get my templates here:

BestSellingAuthorProgram.com/free-module-28-days-to-100k/

Book-A-Month (BAM) Annual Publishing Chart

Title/Subtitle	Genre/Series	Outline/Write	Edited	Cover Design	Proofed	Formatted	Book Description	ISBN	Pub. Date	Launch Date

Chapter 3

Rapid Writing Secrets

Let's face it, getting started writing while staring at a blank page is hard. You either have too many ideas or not enough ideas. I know; I've been there. That's why I created "**16 Rapid Writing Secrets**" to help you get the book out of your head and onto the paper as quickly as possible.

Since our goal is to write books that will be placed in the Short Reads category on Amazon, we can publish a book that has as few as 11 pages (which is crazy) and as many as 99 pages.

Don't be concerned about the number of pages if it is low. People will want to read your book if they feel it will solve their problems. And the faster they learn how to solve the problem, the better.

I buy a lot of Kindle books and there is something very satisfying about watching the percentage of "pages read" increase on my Kindle app as I flip through the eBook. I love buying Short Reads and finishing the book in 1-2 days.

There is a large audience for shorter books, and your monthly books will fit nicely into this Short Reads category.

I have a developed *16 Rapid Writing Secrets* for you. Here are my 4 favorite ones:

1. Start with a powerful quote
2. Write the first paragraph
3. Write it out of sequence
4. Write your book on Post-it Notes

I can honestly say that without these *Rapid Writing Secrets,* I probably wouldn't be able to write a book a month. I love writing out of sequence because it doesn't engage my left brain that wants to put everything in a logical order. I do that AFTER I write the book.

So, let's take a look at ALL of the *16 Rapid Writing Secrets* so you can get this knowledge out of your head and onto the paper:

16 RAPID WRITING SECRETS

1. SPEAK YOUR BOOK

Many of my clients do NOT like to sit down and write. So, I have them record what they want to include in their book and then have the recordings transcribed. An editor or assistant puts all the recordings in cohesive order and creates the book. You can do this yourself by downloading the "Rev" app to your smartphone. Then, create recordings for your book and have them transcribed. This is a very quick way to get your book done!

2. HAVE SOMEONE INTERVIEW YOU

Have someone who isn't familiar with your topic interview you about it. Come up with questions for them to ask you and record the answers and then have them transcribed.

3. WRITE THE FIRST PARAGRAPH

When writing a book, the hardest part is writing the first paragraph. Once it's written, though, the rest will flow. You can even write the first paragraph for each chapter and then go back and add the remaining content. Also, you don't have to write the chapters in the order they will appear in the book. Start with the chapters that you feel the most energy around.

4. WRITE THE CHAPTER SUMMARY FIRST

Many books write themselves once you start writing, so creating a chapter summary will help get the ideas out of your head and give you a place to start.

5. WRITE IN A FRESH ENVIRONMENT

Because of distractions at home, you might get more writing done away from your home office. Go to a coffee shop, your local bookstore, or sit outside, anywhere that you won't be distracted from writing.

6. WRITE IT OUT OF SEQUENCE

Many writers get too focused on the sequence of the chapters and never write anything. That's why you need an editor who will review your book and move things around if they seem out of sequence. Or you can move the chapters around yourself once you've written them all. Don't be too concerned about the order of the chapters because the main goal is to get it out of your head. For me, trying to figure out the sequence as I'm writing slows me down tremendously. Just knowing I can rearrange the chapters when I'm done allows my writing to flow with ease!

7. WRITE WHERE THE EMOTION IS

You should write about a topic you have strong emotion around because it is important to connect with your readers' emotions. Write down ideas that are high on your emotional scale. You've probably heard the saying, "Make Your Mess Your Message." What messes can you write about?

8. WRITE THE STORIES FIRST, THEN MAKE YOUR POINTS

Everyone loves a good story. People easily remember stories more than a list of facts. There is power in the phrase, "Once upon a time…" So, write your stories first, and then add the points.

Method:

1. Write a Story.
2. Make three points.
3. Rinse and Repeat.

That's it!

9. KEEP AN IDEA OR BRAINSTORMING JOURNAL

Once you decide on the book topic, you'll start getting ideas when you're out walking, showering, drinking a cup of coffee or tea, eating a meal, etc. As these ideas come to you, write them in a journal (let your subconscious write your book for you). When we aren't trying to *chase* ideas, they will often come to us effortlessly.

10. TEXT YOUR BOOK TO YOURSELF OR USE THE NOTES APP

When we text others, we get right to the point. Text your book via the "Notes" app on your smart phone instead of sitting in front of a computer staring at a blank page. Sometimes, we need to trick our brain in order to get things done.

11. WRITE YOUR BOOK WITH POST-IT NOTES

I've used this method and it's amazing. You'll need some Post-it Notes and something to stick them on to like a poster board or a white board. Do a brain dump and write everything you can think of about your topic on each Post-it Note. Then, sort them out and group them together around a theme to create the outline for your book.

12. BLOG YOUR BOOK

I have done a couple of books for clients who collected past blog posts they have written. The took the blog posts and edited them, rearranged them, and sometimes added new content to them. Then they repurposed those blog posts into a brand-new book.

13. PODCAST YOUR BOOK

If you have a podcast, transcribe each episode and use it for a book chapter, and voilà, you have a book!

14. POWERPOINT YOUR BOOK

Many people love using PowerPoint to create content, so why not use it to write your book? Create a slide for each topic in your book, then fill it in with more details.

15. START WITH POWERFUL QUOTES

When I see a great quote, I feel inspired. Many books I've read include a powerful quote at the beginning of each chapter. An easy way to get your book started is to collect 10-12 quotes related to your topic and write a chapter based on each of those quotes.

16. WRITE YOUR BOOK WITH BLOCK TIME

We do our best work when we are in a "FLOW" state, which is when we are completely absorbed in the activity at hand (also known as being "in the zone"). To accomplish this:

- Do your highest value work early in the day.
- Set this time aside as your *block time*.

- Don't do any tasks that are distracting beforehand (email, watching the news, scrolling through social media, etc.).

What are your favorite *Rapid Writing Secrets*? Use what works best for you!

Chapter 4

From Mind Dump to Book Outline

After I have a *working title* for my book, I do a four-step mind dump of everything that pops into my mind about this topic.

Step One

Gather your Post-it notes and some colorful sharpies. Once you have an idea about the topic you want to write about and have researched other successful books on that topic, write each idea on a Post-it Note and place them on a large white board.

Step Two

Organize the Post-it Notes into logical groups based on the topic or theme.

Step Three

Remove any that don't fit. Either throw them away or save them for another book. This is the elimination process.

Step Four

Keep removing until you have 4-6 topics for each chapter. Then take those topics and fill out the book creation template shown below to organize writing your book.

Book-A-Month (BAM) Book Creation Template

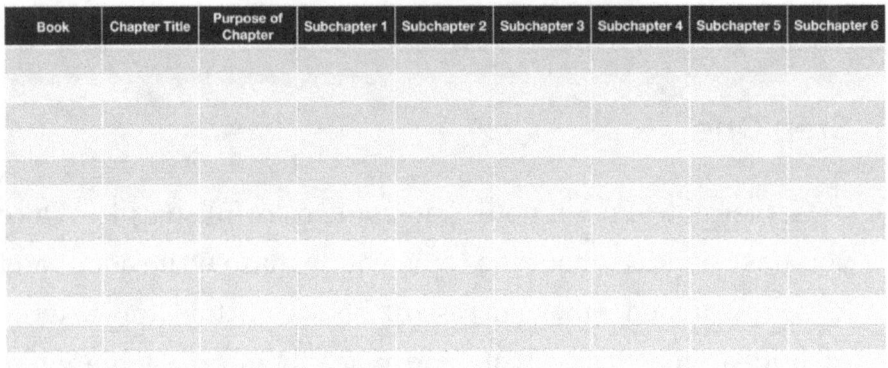

*I have a second page of this template that has a total of 12 chapters on it. Your book might just be six or eight chapters, and that's okay.

Congratulations! Taking these four steps will save you hours of wasted time!

Remember, the goal is to write books that will be placed in the "Short Reads" category on Amazon which is why I don't recommend having more than 12 chapters. A chapter can be just a few pages. Don't add fluff or meandering stories to your book. Just help your reader get the benefit your book promises.

I made the mistake of not using this template while writing some of my books, and it was much more difficult to get organized. Of course, things change as you begin to write (like chapter titles, etc.), but this template will keep you more laser focused with your book. Having your outline before you write your book, will help you flow through the writing process much quicker.

I want to simplify everything for you so you can reach your goal of writing a book a month. Our minds love to complicate things because our self-saboteur doesn't want us to finish our book. We must move past the *resistance* and get our book out to the world!

If you are feeling resistance, pick up a copy of Steven Pressfield's amazing book, "Turning Pro" or "The War of Art." You'll learn that the resistance is real and that you must be vigilant and fight against it.

PRO TIP: Don't tell any close friends or family members about your book. Don't ask their opinion or seek their advice because that can block you.

The only way you know what readers like is by writing, publishing, and launching your book. I call this the "Launch and Learn" method! Then, you will see what the market says by the number of sales you get.

Now that I have published more than six books using this system, I can see which books are doing well and which ones aren't doing as well. I don't take it personally and neither should you. Books are very subjective. Some people will love your books, and some won't. It's okay. Keep writing.

The more you write, the greater success you will have.

Think about playing the lottery. If you buy one ticket, your chances of winning are slim. If you buy 10, 25, or 100 tickets, then your chances just increased.

You don't know and you can't predict which books you write will do well. The market decides. Just put forth your best effort, follow the bestseller checklist and tips in this book, and see what happens. Remember, this is an experiment, and we are here to learn and see what works, and what doesn't.

Also, you may have more than one version of your book. One of the greatest benefits of self-publishing on Amazon is if you need to go back and fix a typo or add something new to your book, it's very easy to do that.

Chapter 5

Seven Questions to Ask Before You Write Your Book

People buy nonfiction books to find a solution to a problem. If you can write your book to just one person who is your ideal reader, then your book will feel very personal and really get inside the reader's mind. Don't try to write a broad book that will appeal to the masses.

Go broad and go broke, or niche and grow rich!

Books that are selling well are niche books that solve a specific problem.

When deciding on the topic and the title of your book, you must answer these seven questions:

1. Who is your audience?

Think about exactly who would buy your book. If you have a business, you can write this book to your ideal clients. Try to be as specific as possible when deciding who you are writing the book for so you can write the book to one person instead of a large group of people.

2. **What Benefits Will People Gain by Reading Your Book?**

List all of the benefits the reader will gain by reading your book. Don't be afraid to be bold when writing this list. For example, "The Backwards Book Launch: Reverse Engineer Your Book and Unlock It's HIDDEN 6-Figure Potential" sends the message that authors who read this book will learn how to make a living with their writing and with their books by reverse engineering the process.

3. **What pain does your ideal reader have?**

Think about the *pain* your reader is experiencing and why they are buying your book. People are not buying their way *into* something as much as they are buying their way *out* of something. What problem is your ideal reader buying their way out of by purchasing your book? Are they broke, sick, looking for a relationship? You must be super clear on how your book helps minimize or eliminate their pain. The biggest areas people seek help in are finances, business, career, health and fitness, and relationships.

4. **What title will best speak to your ideal reader?**

I recommend you come up with at least 5-10 titles. Then, create a survey using a free service like SurveyMonkey to determine the top two titles. The survey results may give you some insight into your next book or what the subtitle the book can be. Make sure that you survey your ideal reader to get the best results.

5. What benefits or pain points can you use in the title or subtitle?

Sometimes, a title doesn't clearly represent the topic of the book. Make sure the subtitle does! The subtitle should tell readers exactly what they will learn from your book and why they should read it.

6. How can you grab the reader's attention with your title?

Gone are the days where you can be "subtle" when coming up with titles. Don't be boring. Some of the best performing books on the market have outrageous titles! For example: "The Subtle Art of Not Giving a F*ck" by Mark Manson; "Love Yourself Like Your Life Depends On It" (the title isn't so outrageous, but the cover on the book shows a silhouette of a man holding a gun to his head with a red heart on his chest and it definitely grabs people's attention); "You are a Badass" by Jen Sincero; "Unlimited Memory" by Kevin Horsley (big claim). You get the picture. Don't be subtle, shy, or low-key. It's a crowded market and you've got to stand out!

7. What keywords can you use in the title or subtitle?

Having one or two of the top keywords for your niche in the title or subtitle of your book will help you get more visibility on Amazon.

Great job!

By taking the time to answer these seven questions, you should have more clarity about who your reader is, what problems they have, and what benefits your book provides to solve their problems.

Keywords

Let's talk a little more about keywords because they are critical to the success of your book.

Readers find books on Amazon's crowded platform by searching for keywords that help them find a book that will solve their problem.

For example, my book, "Backwards Book Launch: Reverse Engineer Your Book to Unlock its Hidden 6-figure Potential", is found with the following seven keywords that I selected (this is the maximum number of keywords allowed when publishing on Amazon KDP):

1. Book Launch
2. 6-Figure Author
3. How to Market a Book
4. Multiple Streams of Income
5. Self-Publishing Books
6. How to Make Money Writing
7. How to Make a Living as a Writer

Selecting your keywords (especially if you have not yet written your book) will help you get clear on your audience and how potential readers on Amazon are searching for information on that particular topic.

I see authors guess what keywords are best for their book, and 99% of the time they are wrong.

The best way to find the right keywords is to first do a brain dump about what you *think* the keywords are for your book; then go to Amazon and type those exact keywords you wrote down in the search bar.

If you start typing these keywords in the search bar on Amazon and the list self-populates, then you know others are searching for those keywords too. If nothing pops up based on the keywords you entered, you should not use those keywords when publishing your book.

I use a paid software program called **Publisher Rocket** to significantly reduce the time spent searching for keywords for my books. Of course, you can manually search for keywords, but it will take longer.

Doing keyword research first can also give you more ideas about what books to write and what to include in your chapters. You can find keywords from the search bar on Amazon and use those keyword phrases as the "exact" title of your book.

My client, Lisa Phillips, used the exact keyword phrase people were searching for on Amazon with great results. Lisa's book sales average $2k to $4k+ every month since her book was published almost two years ago. The title of her book is "Investing in Rental Properties for Beginners."

We tried to come up with a clever book title for Lisa's book, but we decided to just use the keywords people were searching for on Amazon and that turned out to be a great decision since the book is still selling well! Her book also makes her 6-figures on the back end which is awesome.

Knowing your audience and what they are searching for is critical to your success.

Chapter 6

The Bestseller Checklist

This goal isn't just to quickly write and publish a book; the goal is to put out a *high-quality book* that will be launched to the bestsellers list and remain there for a long time. To help do this, I have created a *Bestseller Checklist* for you.

Here's an overview of the Bestseller Checklist:

- Start with the End
- Pound the Payoff
- The Snowflake Hook
- Attached at the Hip
- Cover Judgement
- Ramp Up Reviews
- The Preview Presell
- The Synopsis Cliffhanger
- Know Your Quick Pitch
- Launch Like a Pro

Each item on the checklist is described below. Think of these items as creating a solid foundation for your book.

START WITH THE END

First, pick your profit path strategy. The four biggest authority profit engines from a bestselling book are:

1. Speaking Engagements
2. High-Ticket Coaching
3. Digital Courses
4. Live Events

Many authors earn 6-7 figures on the backend of their books. Think beyond the book—your book is only the beginning. It's often the first introduction people have of you, and it can easily and effortlessly turn a cold lead into a warm lead. When someone reads your book and needs help implementing the strategies you presented, that's your opportunity to help them while you increase the profits from your book. Win-Win!

POUND THE PAYOFF

What's in it for them? If your book is all about you, readers will quickly lose interest. Make sure your title, subtitle, and especially your book description shows the potential reader the IMMENSE benefits they will receive from reading your book.

THE SNOWFLAKE HOOK

No two snowflakes are the same. You must create a book that has NOT been written before. Here are some ideas (with actual book titles as examples):

- **Change the Perspective**: *Public Speaking for People Who Hate Public Speaking*

- **Shock Factor**: *The Subtle Art of Not Giving a F*ck*

- **Create a New Process/Method/System**: *Habit Stacking: 127 Small Changes to Improve Your Health, Wealth and Happiness*

- **Make the Complicated Simple**: *The Index Card: Why Personal Finance Doesn't Have to Be Complicated*

- **Against the Norm**: *The 30-Hour Day: Develop Achiever's Mindset and Habits*

- **Contrary Messaging** – *The Obstacle is the Way*

- **Solve a Million Dollar Problem**: *Profit First: Transform Your Business from a Cash-Eating Monster to a Money-Making Machine*

- **Mimic the Classics** – *Write and Grow Rich*

A good hook grabs the reader's attention and piques interest! Think outside the box.

ATTACHED AT THE HIP

Authors need to be thinking about lifetime followers, NOT only one-time readers. Offer the reader a high-value lead magnet at the beginning of your book and gain a lifetime follower on your email list. Also, start a Facebook group for your readers and include an invitation to join in your book. Then, you can develop a relationship with them inside your private group! And, if you happen to sell something on the backend, these readers and followers now become clients!

COVER JUDGEMENT

Readers do judge books by their cover, so make sure your cover is professional, appealing, and attractive to your target audience.

- Pay a professional.
- Do a design contest on platforms like 99designs.
- Take polls and surveys.
- Learn what your ideal reader likes.

I have a professional designer for all of my books, and I never skimp in this area.

RAMP UP REVIEWS

Good reviews sell books, bad reviews block sales. Getting reviews isn't easy, so put together a private Facebook group (aka your "Street Team") and gather your fans who will be the first to read your book when it comes out and are willing to write a review.

THE PREVIEW PRESELL

Put your best foot forward. Amazon has a "Look Inside" feature also known as the "preview" that allows people considering purchasing a book to view 10% of the eBook's content. Make it Count! Don't fill it with Acknowledgements or lengthy disclaimers. Move that material to the back of the book. Put your best material in the front of your book! The goal is to get people to click the BUY NOW button.

THE SYNOPSIS CLIFFHANGER

Most book descriptions are poorly written because they contain dry facts and give away the contents of the book. Your book description should pique the readers' curiosity and leave them anxious to learn more. The three parts to a great book description are: 1) Identify the problem; 2) Hint at the possible solutions; 3) State why your book is the solution.

KNOW YOUR QUICK PITCH

"You know how _____ (problem)? Well, my book [shows/helps/does] _____ (solves problem), so they _____ (benefit)." Fill in the blanks with your book.

Example: Quick Pitch for the book "How to Make People Like You in 90 Seconds or Less."

Quick Pitch: You know how some people have trouble connecting with others? Well, my book shows you how to do it naturally and easily… so you can be confident and get more out of life.

Knowing your Quick Pitch helps you quickly and easily explain your book to others.

LAUNCH LIKE A PRO

A book launch aims to get to the top of the Bestsellers list and consequently go from being invisible to visible. The bestseller lists are the most searched lists on Amazon which is why they are so important. Once you are on a Bestsellers list, Amazon often promotes your book to its customers! There are several types of launches you can do depending on your goals with your book. For example, you can do free or paid launches, and you can do them for 1-5 days.

****

There you have it! The *Bestseller Checklist* will help you have a well-thought-out book instead of a hasty book that doesn't sell. We want long term sales, not just fast, easy sales when we launch.

Chapter 7

Your 12-Month Plan

I'll admit it, I didn't have a plan when I first started writing a book a month. I just wrote the first book and then the second book and then, in the middle of the night, it came to me that I needed to organize the books for the entire year and decide which genres I wanted to write in.

Let's talk about that for a moment.

Should you write all of your books in the same genre or diversify?

Remember, you can experiment so you don't need to be attached to any one method. You can certainly test writing in different genres to see which of your books do best.

That being said, several authors I know who are making six or seven figures tend to write in one specific genre and are well known for that genre.

One example that comes to mind is Steve Scott who writes under the name S.J. Scott as well. Here's Steve's story:

Steve Scott is the author of over 40+ books and is also an online course creator who makes approximately $30-$50k per month in passive income. When he was struggling to make money online, he was promoting a lot of different affiliate programs.

In 2012, he started writing books and self-publishing on Amazon in the "make money online" space but didn't have very much success at first.

It wasn't until he "niched" down and decided to focus on "habits" that his income grew exponentially. He started his website, www.DevelopGoodHabits.com, and that was the best decision he made because he multiplied his audience and his income in a big way!

It wasn't until he had written several books that one of his books, "Habit Stacking," really took off and he started earning thousands of dollars per month. There are two important lessons here: 1) Your writing gets better the more that you write. 2) You never know which book will take off. Therefore, the more you write, the more success you will ultimately have.

Also, I want to say that Steve Scott has co-authored many books with other successful people. By doing this, he piggy-backs off of their audience and has new people buying his books. This is a great strategy for you to think about down the road.

Ultimately, picking one niche is a good idea. However, when you're starting out, you may not know which books will do well or which genre you have more energy around or which types of books you love writing. So, you will have to test it out.

If you are not going to write in one genre, then my suggestion is to write a series of books for each genre and not just one book.

Here's how this would look:

- 2 genres with 6 books in each genre for 12 months
- 3 genres with 4 books in each genre for 12 months
- 4 genres with 3 books in each genre for 12 months

When I started thinking about which genre and series of books I wanted to write in, here is what I came up with:

- Business/Entrepreneurship
- Career/Passion/Purpose
- Self-Help/Women
- Books for Authors and Writers

These are the topics I have the most knowledge about and it's where my energy and passions are. I do know that it's much easier to "write what you know." I've tried to write books that required a lot of research, but in the BAM (book a month) system, time is not on your side, and you don't have that luxury. So, stick to what you know.

In this chapter, you are going to create your 12-month plan. Before you start planning your titles and books for the year, you must first decide if you want to write in one genre OR you want to mix it up and diversify.

For myself, I like the idea of having four genres and seeing how the books do. Then the following year, I can decide what other books to write based on previous year's results.

So, in which genre(s) do you want to write?

Ideas for Nonfiction Books

Business	Entrepreneurship
Finance	Investing
Women and Business	Marketing
Sales	Accounting
Self Help	Spiritual
Religion	Health
Stress Management	Diets
Weight Loss	Exercise
Nutrition	Sex
Relationships	Marriage
Divorce	Healing
Habits	Travel

Check out the Bestsellers lists and categories on Amazon for more ideas.

Take the time to write out your 12-Month Plan and post it where you can review it daily.

Blank BAM 12-Month Planning Template

Book-A-Month (BAM) Annual Publishing Chart

Title/Subtitle	Genre/Series	Outline/Write	Edited	Cover Design	Proofed	Formatted	Book Description	ISBN	Pub. Date	Launch Date

Sample BAM 12-Month Planning Template

Book-A-Month (BAM) Annual Publishing Chart

Title/Subtitle	Genre/Series	Outline/Write	Edited	Cover Design	Proofed	Formatted	Book Description	ISBN	Pub. Date	Launch Date
Quit Your Job & Follow Your Dreams	Biz/Career								Nov. 2019	Jan. 2020
How to Find Your Passion	Biz/Career								Jan. 2020	Feb. 2020
Work From Home & Make 6 Figures	Biz/Career								Feb. 2020	March 2020
Stop Living Paycheck-to-Paycheck	Biz/Money								March 2020	April 2020
Love Yourself Big	Self-Help/Women								April 2020	May 2020
28 Books to $100K	Biz/Author								May 2020	June 2020
Career Path Rehab	Biz/Career								June 2020	July 2020
Make Money While You Sleep	Biz/Money								July 2020	August 2020
Spandex Habits	Biz/Success								August 2020	Sept. 2020
Digital Retirement	Biz/Money								Sept. 2020	Oct. 2020
Red Dress Energy	Self-Help/Women								Oct. 2020	Nov. 2020
Secrets of Six Figure Women	Biz/Women								Nov. 2020	Dec. 2020

Remember, nothing is set in stone with this plan.

If I start writing a book and I'm just not "feeling" it, then I'll change directions. Maybe I'll work on one of the other books from my list, or maybe I'll come up with a new idea.

If you get stuck, find some old content that you can repurpose. For years, I created and sold several online courses. One of those courses is, "Make Money While You Sleep," which is about creating online courses – this happens to be an online course I taught and sold years ago that I have now updated and repurposed into a brand-new book!

As I mentioned earlier, if you've written some blog posts that can be repurposed into a book, that's a great shortcut as well. The same can be done with podcasts – select your best shows and use each one as a chapter for your book.

Follow your intuition and guidance and then write where your energy is. Of course, you want to balance that out with doing your keyword research and making sure there is a demand for the type of book you are writing. If you skip this step, then you probably won't earn any income from the book because there is simply not a market for it.

In his book, "Write to Market," author Chris Fox says, "There are two methods of writing a book. You can write, then market. Or you can write to market. One has a much, much higher chance of success than the other. The first method is writing whatever pops into your head…most likely it will result in your writing a book that almost no one reads. Harsh, but accurate. Writing to market is picking an under-served genre that you know has a voracious appetite, and then giving that market exactly what it wants."

Chris Fox has written several fiction books, but he also has a series of nonfiction books for authors.

I do believe there is a lot of truth to what he is saying.

When I am "thinking" about a topic for my book, the first thing I do is open *Publisher Rocket* and do my keyword research. If I find that the topic of my book has good "search volume" and good "average monthly earnings," then I will proceed. If the search volume is low and the earnings are low, then I do not proceed.

I'll come up with 5-10 keywords to research and then decide.

Below is an example of the keywords and search volume for my book "How to Find Your Passion" I found using *Publisher Rocket* when I was researching the topic:

Keywords	Searches
How to find the work you love	5,250
How to find your calling in life	1238
How to find your purpose and do what you love	973
How to find your purpose in life	488
How to find your passion	252
Discover your true north	390

Based on those numbers, I felt it was a good topic to write about, and also one for which I have a lot of energy around. It happens to be my top income producing book as well!

Don't just write what pops into your head. Do your research, and then plan out your books for 12 months.

Chapter 8

Self-Publishing 101

This is not a book on all the details of self-publishing like how to format a book, etc. This chapter gives you a general overview of the important steps in the self-publishing process. I use the following Self-Publishing checklist with my clients in my Bestseller program.

You can use this Self-Publishing Checklist to keep you organized and to be successful:

- Finalize your manuscript.
- Have your manuscript edited.
- Review changes with *track changes* enabled in Microsoft Word so you can accept or reject changes.
- Set the manuscript aside for 2-3 days if you have time. Then, read through it again word-for-word to see if anything was missed and fix it. Also, make any last-minute changes.
- Have the manuscript formatted for both an eBook and print book. *My editor is also my formatter, which is super helpful.
- Decide on your title and subtitle. If you are stuck, do a title survey with SurveyMonkey which is a free service.

- Once you have finalized your title, then purchase your ISBN number for the print book (you don't need an ISBN for the eBook). ISBNs cost $125 for one or $299 for a block of ten on Bowker.com. I usually purchase a block of ten since I am writing a book a month, I know I'm going to use them. Make sure you give the ISBN to your editor to be added to your copyright page.

- I created a publishing company for my books, Monarch Crown Publishing, which is part of my business LLC. I register my books under this name because if I want to speak at book festivals or other events, some of those venues don't accept self-published authors; this is sort of a loophole around this rule.

- Get your cover done. You might want to wait until after you finalize the manuscript because the title and/or subtitle may change. I usually get three mockups done and pick the one I love the most, then finalize. For the eBook, you will use the front cover only. The print cover cannot be finalized until you know the following three things:

    1) The trim size of the book (I usually do 6x9),

    2) Paper color (on Amazon, you can choose between white and cream paper. Each type has a different thickness which will affect the spine of your cover.) I always select white paper for my books.

    3) The page count of your print book.

I also have my designer create 3D cover mockups that I can use for marketing.

- Document your category and keywords research. I create a Word document called "categories and keywords" for each book and list the categories and the seven keywords I selected for that book.

- Use the keywords to create Amazon Ads or share them with someone you hire to create the ads for you.

- When you publish your book, Amazon only allows you to select two categories. Once your book is published, you can submit a support ticket to Amazon's customer service and request your book be included in 6-8 additional categories. If you are having a hard time finding categories, there is a paid software I used called, "Bestseller Ranking Pro."

- Write your book description. If you are not good at writing "sales copy," then you might want to hire a copywriter. Bryan Cohen offers a service where he will write an amazing book description for you. You can find him at: BestPageForward.net/Blurbs

- Have your final book description formatted with html tags for headings, bold and italic text, and bullet lists, so it looks nice on your Amazon book detail page. I use this free service by Dave Chesson through his Kindlepreneur site:

    Kindlepreneur.com/Amazon-Book-Description-Generator

- The book description will also be included on the back cover of your book. I also include an author photo and a short bio.

- Add a call to action at the end of the book description for the Amazon book page. For example, on the Amazon book page for my book, "Stop Living Paycheck to Paycheck," the last paragraph says, "If you're ready to take control of your finances and get prepared for those rainy days, click the BUY NOW button and join Michelle on your journey to Financial Freedom."

- Publish your eBook and print book on Amazon. It doesn't matter which one you do first. I usually set up the eBook first because it takes me more time to get everything ready for the print version. Also, that allows me to start getting the five reviews I need to do a book launch. I talk more about hiring promoters for your launch in the "Launch Like a Pro" Chapter. Just know that most book promoters you hire will NOT accept your book without five, and sometimes ten, reviews.

- Set up your Amazon Author Central page, which is your bio page where you can list all of the books you have published on Amazon. You can also include any editorial reviews you have there.

- Amazon will link your eBook and print versions so they appear on the same page. If the versions are not linked within a few days of publishing, you can email Amazon customer support for help or connect them through Author Central.

- Get your 5-10 reviews.

- Schedule two-day launch dates. I usually select either:

    Tuesday/Wednesday
    Wednesday/Thursday
    Thursday/Friday.

- Hire the book promoters and decide what type of launch you are doing: free or discounted at .99. If you do a free promotion, make sure you set up those dates in your KDP account. (I go over the launch details in the Launch Like a Pro chapter.)

- Set up your social media posts for Facebook, Twitter, LinkedIn, Instagram, etc. to run on those two days. I use Hootsuite which allows me to set up my social media posts in advance.

- On the day of your launch, promote the book in an email to your mailing list if you have one.

- On the day of the launch, you should check the Amazon bestseller lists every few hours and take screenshots as your book moves up in the rankings.

- Once you reach #1 on the bestsellers list(s), you can add the #1 Amazon bestseller logo to your cover, if desired.

- Create a marketing collage (I use a free software called PicMonkey) using the screen shots from your best seller campaign and share on social media to express how excited you are about your book.

- After the launch, increase the price of the eBook; or if you want, leave it at .99 for one week to see how it maintains on the bestsellers lists.

- Set up Amazon ads for more rocket fuel for your book (more on this in a separate chapter).

- Set up at least two media interviews for more exposure (more on this in a separate chapter).

- Rinse and Repeat!

I know it sounds like a lot, but I do it every month, and after a couple of launches, you'll be a pro, too!

Chapter 9

Launch Like a Pro

I like to break down my book launches into three phases:

1. Pre-Launch
2. Launch
3. Post-Launch

A book launch is simply a designated time period in which you put all of your book marketing efforts to get a lot of sales (or downloads) of your book.

The goal of a book launch is to get the highest number of sales/downloads in the shortest amount of time so your book will hit the bestseller lists. We will talk more about how to consistently stay on bestseller lists, but the first goal is to reach the bestseller lists.

How to "Launch" Your Book...

You can either promote your book for free for two days by signing up for Amazon's KDP select, in which you agree to publish your book exclusively with Amazon for 90 days. In exchange, Amazon will provide you with two promotional tools: *free days* and *countdown days*. For our purposes, we are only focused on free days so you would use the *free days* tool to give your book away for free for two days.

FREE Book Launches

Why give away your book for free?

To get your book in the hands of potentially thousands of people will read your book, write reviews, create buzz, and trigger the Amazon algorithm. I find that most nonfiction books end up on the paid bestsellers list organically after I do a free launch.

Book Launches with Discounted Prices

If you have a large social media following and/or email list, then you do NOT need to do a free launch. Instead, discount your eBook to .99 cents and do a "paid" 1 or 2-day launch. During a paid 1 to 2-day launch, you will sell 50-500+ books. Every book is different so I can't say exactly how many books you will sell. It also depends on if you have a big email lists, how big your social media following is and how many book promoters you hire during your launch.

I want to mention royalties; if you price your eBook between $2.99 and $9.99, then you will earn 70% in royalties. If your eBook is priced under $2.99 or over $9.99, then you will only earn 35% in royalties.

Obviously, you are not making money on a free launch, but your book will have wider exposure and will most likely go to the paid bestsellers list immediately following the free launch and start making paid sales.

Because I have a large email list and following, I do paid launches for all of my books. I set the price for my book to .99 for the launch days, hire paid promoters, and send it out to my email list and post on social media as well. At midnight on the second day of the launch, I set the eBook price to $2.99, and I find that I get a lot of sales after that at the full price making 70% royalties (which is about $2.00 for a $2.99 eBook).

The BIG goal here is to get to as many paid bestsellers lists as you can, because these are the most searched lists on Amazon and that's where your readers can discover YOUR BOOK!

LAUNCH CHECKLIST

PRE-LAUNCH

- Research your keywords and use them in your title, subtitle, and book description; as I talked about previously, keywords are the words people type in the search bar on Amazon to find your book.
- 30 days prior to your launch, start posting updates on social media about your upcoming book to warm up the audience; write a blog post if you have a blog.
- Create 5-10 titles for your book and do a survey using SurveyMonkey to select the best title. If you're not stuck with the title, then you can skip this step.
- Have 2-3 concepts of your book cover made and post them on social media asking friends and followers to vote for their favorite.

- Decide on a FREE gift (lead magnet) to give away with your book to help build your email list. Create a landing page for readers to download or access the free gift.

- Upload your book about 1-2 weeks prior to the launch so you have time to get at least five reviews (the more the better) before you hire the book promoters. I call this a "soft launch." Don't upload your book too far in advance of your launch because you can only get on the Amazon "**Hot New Releases**" list within 30 days of publishing your book.

- Once your book is uploaded and has been reviewed and approved by Amazon, then you can start getting reviews.

- Price your eBook at .99 because it will be easier to get reviews at this price point.

- Reach out to influencers (press, bloggers, or podcasters) and ask them to promote your book during the launch.

- Send a PDF copy of your book to industry influencers for reviews.

- Create a Facebook event and let friends and friends of friends know about your book launch.

- Write emails to be sent out to your subscribers during launch week.

- If you are doing a video trailer (which should include your free dates if yours is a free launch), post it on YouTube two to four weeks before your launch and promote it. If the book will be discounted to .99 for the launch, include that information in your video trailer.

- Upload your eBook to Amazon KDP and select two DIFFERENT categories to put your book in when publishing.

- After your eBook is published, do more extensive category research and add 6-8 more categories in which your book can rank high. This is very important because it allows you to diversify your audience and rank #1 on multiple bestsellers lists. You will need to submit a customer support ticket to Amazon to request placement in the additional categories.

- When publishing your book, make sure to use all seven keywords permitted by Amazon based on your research.

- Submit your book to the book promotion sites about two weeks before your promo starts. I usually hire 5-10 promoters for the launch which costs around $200+.

- Note: some promoters only accept promotions for free books, and some only accept paid promotions. Therefore, be aware when hiring promoters and confirm they can do the type of promotion you are looking for. Some of the promoters I use are listed in the Resources section of this book.

- If you are doing press releases, submit your press releases or pay somebody on fiverr.com to submit your press release to some PR sites.

LAUNCH

- If you are doing a free or discounted (paid) launch, keep your book priced at .99 cents.

- If you have a large email list and following, then do a discounted paid launch at .99 for two days.

- Post to social media (Twitter, Facebook, LinkedIn, Instagram, etc.) daily or hourly during the launch. I use Hootsuite and schedule posts with photos of the book, hashtags, and a link to the book on Amazon in advance that go out several times during the launch.

- Email your list on each day of the launch.

- Be sure to thank everyone who shares, reviews, buys, or supports your book in any way.

- Check your rankings on Amazon and take screen shots as your book rises in the Bestsellers List. Be sure to check international Bestsellers lists as well. Create a document that has links to each category your book is placed on. This will save you a lot of time on launch day.

- Amazon only shows three bestseller categories on your product page, but your book will most likely be on 10-20 bestsellers lists if you selected the right categories. Remember you need to look at the subcategory you chose, and then check the main categories as well.

- Create a marketing collage using a free service like PicMonkey and share your bestseller results on social media.

- Do a two-day FREE launch of your book (unless you have a large email list). The free launch will get you more downloads and potentially add more people to your mailing list if you include a free gift offer at the front of your book.

POST LAUNCH

- Continue to market your book once you are a #1 Amazon Bestselling Author; this is not a one-and-done event.

- Immediately set up Amazon Ads after the launch with at least 500 – 1,000 keywords. This is critical to the success of your book once the launch is over.

- Add the bestseller logo to your cover and resubmit to Amazon (it can take 12-48 hours for approval).

- Immediately set up media interviews once you become a bestselling author.

- Ask for more reviews of your book from people who downloaded it for free (especially if you have an email list.)

- If you did the FREE launch, and your book is not at the top of the paid bestsellers list after it is over; do a paid promotion and hire paid promoters to bump your book up even higher on the bestsellers lists.

- Book Bub is great book promotion service for authors; however, you should know that they reject a lot of books. Also, you have to wait 90 days after you do your own launch before you can submit your book to them. They have over 4 million subscribers and can guarantee sales of your book. One of my clients did a Book Bub promotion and had more than 30,000 downloads of her book in 3 days from that one promotion. You have nothing to lose if you try and get a Book Bub promotion for even more exposure and sales!

- If you don't get accepted by Bookbub.com, then try Ereadernewstoday.com or RobinReads.com.

- I recommend hiring promoters every 60-90 days to maintain your position on the bestsellers list.

- Put 3D mockups of your book cover and links to your bestselling book on the home page of your website (if you have one.)

- Add something about your book to your autoresponder series so you are continually marketing your book to your list.

This is the system I teach to my students and use for my own book launches.

I recently did a paid book launch for the book I published last month and priced it at .99. I hit over a dozen bestsellers list and four of those were #1! Today, I had over 200 sales coming off the .99 2-day launch. I increased the price to $2.99 as soon as that 2-day launch was over. Because I have so many books now, I feel that I can still stay on the top of the paid best sellers lists at $2.99. Eventually, I raise the eBook price to $4.99 if the book is staying on the bestseller lists.

However, if you feel like your book rankings dropped suddenly, then leave it at .99 until it stabilizes on the paid best-sellers list and until your Amazon Ads gain traction.

It's very important that you do a book launch.

Don't make the mistake many authors do by thinking after hitting the "publish" button, readers will magically find your book. I can tell you, with 100% certainty, that until I do the launch, I don't see the increase of my monthly sales for that book. The book is basically invisible on Amazon without a bestseller launch.

DO NOT SKIP THIS STEP!

Chapter 10

Extra Rocket Fuel for Your Book

Marc Reklau, who is a friend and fellow author, has written several bestselling books and is ranked in the top 100 of all authors on Amazon; he told me that he is set to make $31k in royalties this month.

Marc is all about Amazon Ads, and that is what he attributes his huge success to. He started out just like you and I are, and he went from earning a few hundred dollars a month to a few thousand a month to $5k, then $10k, then $20k, and now he's on target to do $31K this month! Crazy!

I'm so happy for his success. He is a great motivation to me and my writing business!

You can check out his books on Amazon at www.Amazon.com/Marc-Reklau/e/B00IZALH04/

Most authors unfortunately don't invest in Amazon ads, and, therefore, their books lack sales and visibility.

Writing, publishing, and launching a book is very important. But if you don't add the fuel to the fire with Amazon ads, then your book will eventually lose visibility on Amazon.

In 2015, I tripled my Bestselling Author done-for-you business by creating PAID Facebook ads that went to an automated webinar to generate leads to a strategy session call. I knew nothing about the Facebook ads platform, but I knew I had to learn it if I wanted to grow my business. That is what I did.

I can assure you that Amazon ads is much easier to learn than Facebook ads, and once you get the hang of it, you only need to spend an hour each day or a few hours per week to have great results.

With $31k in royalties, Marc is probably spending $7-$10k in ad spend – but the point is, it takes money to make money.

Most first-time authors can't invest this much money on Amazon ads, but you can get started with campaigns for as little as $5 per day.

I added this chapter not to teach you the exact steps to set up your Amazon ads (because that would be hard to teach in one chapter), but to give you an introduction to Amazon ads.

My advice to you is – don't abandon your baby after you put all the work into writing, editing, formatting, publishing, and launching your book. Set up Amazon ads and get the visibility your book deserves to generate more sales!

MEDIA INTERVIEWS

Media interviews are a great way to get more buyers for your book.

Nancy Hartwell, my first client in 2013, has now done over 600 interviews. She wrote a fiction book, "Harem Slave," which we published and launched in April of 2013. The topic of that book is human sex slave trafficking, and Nancy has become an expert on this topic. Because of all the media interviews, her book has stayed in the top 10 of the bestsellers lists for seven years now! That's incredible!

In fact, the day after one radio interview, Nancy had 700 downloads of her book! Her eBook sells for $5.99 on Amazon and she gets 70% royalty. So, a 1-hour interview generated $2,933 in royalties for Nancy!

Reach out to podcasters and radio show hosts to be an expert guest on their show once you become a #1 bestseller.

My good friend and fellow author, Marc Guberti, who is a marketing genius, has a podcast show called "Breakthrough to Success" where is has interviewed some amazing authors like: Seth Godin, Neil Patel, John Lee Dumas, James Clear, Perry Marshall and more!

I send all of my clients to him once they become a bestseller to apply to be on his Breakthrough Success podcast: https://marcguberti.com/breakthrough-success-podcast/

Marc Guberti is a USA Today and Wall Street Journal best-selling author with over 100,000 students in over 180 countries enrolled in his online courses. He is a serial podcaster and hosts several virtual summits.

His podcasts include: *Breakthrough Success Podcast, Profitable Public Speaking Podcast,* and *Ditch The Job Podcast.*

Marc published more than 25 books before graduating college and believes that age is not a limit to success.

Marc is a master at leveraging podcasts and virtual summits to drive more sales to his books, courses, and coaching. You can visit him at: MarcGuberti.com.

What are you going to do after you launch your book?

Amazon ads and media interviews are the best ways to drive more sales.

Chapter 11

Income Goals and Income Tracking Chart

What are your personal income goals?

I want to make six figures in passive income from my books, and I won't stop till I get there.

You can determine your income goals based on your current needs. As I said in the introduction, maybe you just want enough to make a car payment, cover a few of your living expenses, or pay your rent or mortgage.

I have found that setting small incremental income goals works well and really motivates me each month as I see my income growing!

Here's the template I use, that you can copy and use as well:

Book-A-Month (BAM) Income Tracking Chart

Month	Book Title	Monthly Income	Date Paid by Amazon	Running Total

I wasn't sure how this would all work, so I decided to set quarterly income goals so I could use the royalties to pay some of my living expenses and bills. The ultimate goal is to make six figures, but I wanted to get quick wins and feel good about all the time and effort I was investing in this project. Each time I hit an income goal, I get super motivated!

Year 1 Income Goals

BAM Income Goals – Michelle Kulp

Goal 1: Make Car Payment with Royalties
– Hit Goal in April 2020 ($392/mo.)

Goal 2: Pay Car Payment, Auto Insurance and Cell Phone
– Hit goal in May 2020 ($664/mo.)

Goal 3: Pay Car Payment, Auto Insurance, Cell Phone, Cable/Internet, and Groceries
– Hit goal in July 2020 ($1400/mo.)

Goal 4: Pay House Payment with Royalties
– Hit goal in September 2020 ($2000/mo.)

Goal 5: Pay all Living Expenses with Royalties - $4000/mo.
– Should hit this goal in Quarter 1 of 2021

I suggest you set quarterly goals instead of monthly goals because there is always a "lag" with your income doing this system.

The reason is twofold:

1. Amazon pays out royalties after 60 days. After you receive the first royalty payment, then royalties are paid every 30 days.

2. When you first publish your book, there is very little income because you have not yet done a book launch or run Amazon ads. Therefore, no one knows about your book, and it is basically invisible on Amazon.

Royalty Payment Example:

- Month 1: Write and publish book 1.
- Month 2: Get five reviews for book 1, set up book promoters, change categories, do 2-day launch for book 1. You are also writing and publishing book 2 in month 2.
- Month 3: Get five reviews for book 2, set up book promoters, change categories, do 2-day launch for book 2. You are also writing and publishing book 3 in month 3.

It's important to note that until you do the launch, you won't have much or any income from that book. Most authors don't do launches, don't get on bestsellers lists, don't get visibility on Amazon and, therefore, don't make much money.

It's important to follow my system if you want to be successful and hit your income goals, whatever they may be.

When I was a single mother of three struggling to make ends meet and living paycheck-to-paycheck, a passive income of $500 or $1000 per month would have been life changing! Unfortunately, I was working a 9-5 job in the legal field with a single stream of income. I wish I had known about this system then.

This "write a book a month" system to create passive income can change your life. It doesn't have to be six figures; it can be whatever you want it to be!

As I mentioned in the introduction, in just 12 months I've been able to create over $3,300 a month in income from writing one short book a month! My goal is to hit six figures in the next 12-18 months!

This is incredible to me especially when I think about what I'll be receiving from social security when I'm old enough to collect (10 years from now) after working 17 long years in the legal field as a paralegal; my social security will be somewhere around $2000 per month. I've already exceeded that amount in just 12 months. That's why you need to start now and create your own financial future.

Seeing your royalty payments increase every month will motivate you to keep going. Of course, there is also the internal reward you will have from having more impact in the world with your message and your teachings from your books!

Set your income goals now and don't give up until you hit them!

Chapter 12

The 30-Day Roadmap to Writing a Book a Month

Now that I've given you the tools, software, templates, tracking charts, fill-in-the-blank title generator, checklists, and everything you need to be successful, I want to give you one last thing – the 30-Day Roadmap for writing a book a month.

It's been a trial-and-error process for me. In the beginning, I didn't have many of the tools, templates, and checklists that I've given you, so I struggled. I saw right away that I needed to be better organized and I developed these out of necessity.

If you take the time to plan out your entire year with the genres and the working title for each month – then on day 1 of each new month, you can start writing that month's book.

So, what is the best way to write? Daily, on weekends, early in the morning, late at night, in blocks of time?

I've tried them all.

I would write every morning when I first woke up until my daughter and 2-year-old granddaughter came to live with me, which changed my "quiet" writing time and schedule.

I find writing a book in 3-7 days works best for me for a few reasons:

1. I easily lose my train of thought. If I write for an hour or two each day, and then don't get back to it for a day or two, I'm completely lost about what I was writing about or where I was heading.

2. Because I run a 6-figure business with multiple programs (www.bestsellingauthorprogram.com), it's hard to balance working with clients every day, taking care of personal things, and writing my book.

3. I like having designated writing days without any client work or tasks so that I can focus solely on my book. I wrote this book in three days. Of course, I did the pre-work, and I used some of my rapid writing secrets that I shared with you earlier. I wrote each chapter and then put them in order after all 12 chapters were written.

PRO TIP: Don't edit when you are in the writing/creating process. That will slow you down significantly. Just get it out of your head and onto the paper. You can clean it up later or have a good editor help you.

Find the writing schedule that works best for you.

I have an amazing client, Dr. Jeffrey Donner, whom I admire a lot. He has a full-time practice as a psychologist and has written six books so far which I've helped him launch to the #1 best sellers list. He writes every evening from 10 pm to 2 am. He also writes a lot while on vacations in Mexico!

That's what works for him.

We are all different and we have different circumstances in our lives, so I don't believe there is a one-size-fits-all method on how to *write a book a month*.

I can get an entire book done when I have uninterrupted time, but that's not always possible for everyone.

In his book, "Deep Work," Cal Newport mentions author Neal Stephenson, who has no email address or contact information on his website. Stephenson said, "If I organize my life in such a way that I get long consecutive uninterrupted time-chunks, I can write novels. [If I instead get interrupted a lot] what replaces it? Instead of a novel that will be around for a long time…there is a bunch of email messages that I have sent out to individual persons."

J.K. Rowling was absent from social media while she wrote the Harry Potter novels.

Woody Allen, who wrote and directed 44 films between 1969 and 2013, never owned a computer. He wrote on a manual typewriter.

Mark Twain wrote much of "The Adventures of Tom Sawyer" in a shed on the property of the Quarry Farm in NY, where he was spending the summer. Twain's study was isolated from the main house, so his family took to blowing a horn to let him know his meals were ready.

Carl Jung built a retreat in the woods he called "The Tower," which was a basic two-story stone house that no one was allowed to enter without his express permission. Jung would rise every day at 7 am and, after breakfast, he would spend two hours of undistracted writing time in his private office. His afternoons consisted of long walks and meditation. Also, there was no electricity in the Tower. Jung retreated to the Tower not to escape his professional life as a psychologist, but to advance it.

We need undistracted time to do our deep work and deep thinking.

Cal Newport talks about the difference between deep work and shallow work, and he defines shallow work as: "Non-cognitively demanding, logistical-style tasks, often performed while distracted. These efforts tend to not create much new value in the world and are easy to replicate."

Conversely, DEEP WORK is: "Professional activities performed in a state of distraction-free concentration that push your cognitive capabilities to their limit. These efforts create new value, improve your skill, and are hard to replicate."

Deep work is a burden to prioritize, but if we want to write high-quality books that can potentially change lives, we need to find and prioritize that time.

Also, we are creating our own economy with our books.

Instead of being dependent on a job, imagine how it would feel if you could make a living with your writing!

I've had to remove a lot of distractions in my life in order to write a book a month.

- Checking email throughout the day – now I only do this twice a day.
- Continually scrolling through my Facebook feed – now I only check it once or twice a day.
- Binge watching TV shows on Netflix.
- Spending time with low-goal or no-goal friends.

What are your go-to distractions that keep you from doing deep work?

- Relationships with a lot of drama
- Reading
- Consuming content (webinars, books, trainings)
- Alcohol and partying
- Emails
- Social media
- Spending time with friends who are not evolving and growing

- Watching sports
- Binge watching shows
- Work-a-holism
- Anything that prevents you from creating art

If you find yourself making excuses that you can't do this because you don't have the time, then start removing some of the above distractions and you will find the time.

If your life depended on writing a book a month, you could do it.

Here's what my 30-day schedule looks like:

Days 1-15

1. Write and organize the book.
2. Wait a few days, then review.
3. Keep Post-it Notes on the project folder when I think of anything to add or remove or notes to send my editor/formatter.

Days 16-23

1. Send the manuscript to editor for initial edits.
2. She returns to me, and I review and accept or reject the changes.
3. The manuscript is sent back to the editor for final formatting.

4. I then read the newly formatted and edited book word-for-word to catch anything we may have missed in the initial review.
5. While she and I are working on the manuscript, my cover designer is working on the cover.

Days 17-30

1. Write the book description, research the keywords and categories, and publish the book.
2. Do a soft launch to get 5-10 reviews.

Following Month

1. Launch the book
2. Start writing the next book.

Closing Thoughts

What are your dreams? Do you dream of being financially independent? Do you dream of being able to pay all of your living expenses from your royalties? Do you dream of having freedom to spend your time how you wish?

Those are my dreams, too, and I support you in your dreams, which is why I have written this book for authors. I believe in authors, and I believe in YOU!

If you want to achieve your dreams, you must plan your time and prioritize your work.

So many times we want the "result," but we don't plan or prioritize our time. This system requires advanced planning and prioritizing in order for it to work.

My goals are not only financial. I also want to help thousands of authors reach their dreams and goals. If I help authors reach their goals, then their books have the power and potential to change someone's life.

Knowing your BIG why will motivate you on those days when you don't *feel* like writing.

What's your BIG why?

- Self-Expression
- Getting Your Message Out to the World

- Leaving a Legacy
- Creating financial independence for yourself and your family
- Being in control of your time
- Doing what you love and getting paid for it

I hope you will join me on this journey to writing a book a month and create more financial freedom in your life so you can achieve all of your audacious dreams!

Several of my clients are doing this process with me and it's working for them as well.

CONECT WITH ME ON FACEBOOK:

Please join our community here:

Facebook.com/groups/28BooksTo100K/

I wish you well on your journey to becoming a successful author, changing the world with your books, and living your dreams!

Michelle Kulp

Bonus

Michelle's Private and Vetted Rolodex

It can take years to find great book promoters, formatters, editors, and cover designers. I currently use the following resources for my books, or these have been recommended to me by other authors.

PROMOTERS: PAID VS. FREE

It's important to understand that there are promoters who will only promote your book when it is free (which you can do by signing up for Amazon's Kindle Select program inside your KDP account) and there are other promoters who only do paid (which typically means your book price is reduced to $.99). Last, there are some promoters that do free and paid launches. I just wanted to point this out.

Promoters for FREE Book Launches

- RobinReads.com/genre-divide/
- BookTweeters.com/#home
- eReaderIQ.com/authors/submissions/dds/
- Fiverr.com/bknights
- JamesHMayfield.com/book-promotions/ *only does free
- FreeBooksy.com/freebooksy-feature-pricing/m

Promoters for Books Priced at Least $.99

***Instead of freebooksy, hire bargainbooksy:

- BargainBooksy.com/sell-more-books-2/
- BookSends.com/advertise.php
- eReaderNewsToday.com/bargain-and-free-book-submissions/#toggle-id-1 *****must be submitted 10-14 days in advance!

*90 days after you do a #1 book launch, you can apply for a BookBub featured deal:

- BookBub Featured Deal, Price Varies: BookBub.com/partners/pricing

**If you don't get accepted, try running ads on their platform:

- BookBub Ads Anytime, Price Varies: Insights. https://www.bookbub.com/partners/bookbub_ads

BOOK COVER DESIGNERS

- 99designs.com/ebook-cover-design
- 100covers.com
- FosterCovers.com
- GraceMyCanvas.com
- Archangelink.com/book-covers/
- FionaJaydeMedia.com/non-fiction/

- Fiverr.com/designa2z
- Fiverr.com/cal5086
- Fiverr.com/galuhh
- Fiverr.com/lauria
- Fiverr.com/vikiana
- Fiverr.com/germancreative
- My designer is Zeljka: vukojeviczeljka@gmail.com

FORMATTERS

- **Heather Mize at My Book Team**
  heather@MyBookTeam.com

TEMPLATES:

For DIY formatting, you can get some great templates at BookDesignTemplates.com

EDITORS (All editors I have used)

- **Heather Mize** – heather@MyBookTeam.com
- **Lori Duff, Esq** – lori@loriduffwrites.com
- **Pamela Gossiaux** – pam@pamelagossiaux.com
- **Hollace Donner** – Pailmoritz@yahoo.com

PROOFREADER

- Kimberly Marzullo – kimberlymarzullo@icloud.com

GHOSTWRITERS

- **Lori Duff, Esq.** – LoriDuffWrites.com/lori-writes-for-you-expert-ghost-writer/ghost-writing-rates
- **Emily Crookston, Ph.D.** – ThePocketPHD.com

COPYWRITERS

- Rob Schultz – ProfitSeduction.com
- BestPageForward.net/blurbs

ONLINE COURSE PLATFORM

- **I use Thinkific** for my "Client Learning Portal," which is essentially my online course/program/training: http://try.thinkific.com/michellekulp6975

PUBLIC RELATIONS

- **Christina Daves** – www.ChristinaDaves.com

SOFTWARE I USE

- *****Aweber:** http://michellekulp.aweber.com
- *****Bluehost:** http://www.bluehost.com/track/mkulp
- *****Pop-Up domination:** https://app.popupdomination.com/aff/5d4a184df5895d7c596f5242
- *****Publisher Rocket** https://mkulp--rocket.thrivecart.com/publisher-rocket/

- **KDSpy**
  https://mkulp--leadsclick.thrivecart.com/kdspy-v5
- **Bestseller Ranking Pro:**
  https://mkulp--tckpublishing.thrivecart.com/bestseller-ranking-pro-special-lifetime/
- **Book Report**: https://app.getbookreport.com/
- **HTML Book Description Generator**:
  https://kindlepreneur.com/amazon-book-description-generator/

BOOK PRINTERS:

- http://www.printopya.com/book

ILLUSTRATORS

- www.Gemini-h.com/illustrations
- www.Instagram.com/art_of_geminih

Note: Some of the links listed above are affiliate links, which means I may receive a commission at no cost to you if you purchase from those link

Notes

www.ingramcontent.com/pod-product-compliance
Lightning Source LLC
LaVergne TN
LVHW051829080426
835512LV00018B/2789